TIME HAPPENS

HAPPENS

YOU COULDN'T HAVE PICKED A BETTER TIME TO BE FIFTYSOMETHING

H. SAMM COOMBS

HALO BOOKS
SAN FRANCISCO

Published by

HALO BOOKS

Post Office Box 2529
San Francisco, CA 94126

Printed in the United States of America

Cover Design: Susan Larson
Text Design and Typesetting: Diane Spencer Hume

Library of Congress Catalog Card Number: 94-34061

Library of Congress Cataloging-in-Publication Data

Coombs, H. Samm, 1928–
    Time happens : you couldn't have picked a better time to be
fiftysomething / H. Samm Coombs.
      p. cm.
    ISBN 1–879904–13–6 (pbk.)
    1. Aged--United States--Psychology.   2. Aging--United States--
Psychological aspects.   3. Aging--United States--Religious
aspects.   4. New Age Movement.   I. Title.
HQ1064.U5C6123   1995
305.26'0973--dc20
                                                                94–34061
                                                                      CIP

Current Edition's most recent printing is indicated by the first digit below:
2   3   4   5   6   7   8   9   0

Shirley, Jefferson, Maureen, Bridget,
and a certain long-suffering Geotechnic Engineer

AND NOW FOR SOMETHING
COMPLETELY DIFFERENT

—Monty Python

CONTENTS

INTRODUCTION

Why a book about the 'frantic fifties?' Because this is life's most neglected and least understood decade. Nothing you've learned to date has prepared you for what's coming.

Libraries are stuffed with learned volumes about *being old,* but little about the threshold years; the process of becoming.

While previous life cycles have been noteworthy in their own way, not even the much-discussed 'mid-life crisis' produces the potential for trauma encountered when you exit middle-age. When this transition is undertaken blindfolded, in a state of denial, you are liable to arrive on the senior side of life with a chip on your shoulder and a pocket full of rocks.

As an early chapter explains, the next two or three decades can be the most confining and monochromatic of your life, or the most colorful and expansive. *It all depends on the attitude you adopt in your fifties.*

The right attitude is the sum of many parts, each to its own chapter: the irrelevance of chronological age; how to relieve your self of resentments and regrets collected on the way to fifty; taking your parents place at The Edge; the problem with problems and how to make less of more; a technique of making the rest of your life a series of beginnings; avoiding the inertia syndrome; some unconventional wisdom about your health; how to let go of what's weighing you down, and, finally, why this time of life is the perfect time to take risks.

All of this will challenge, to some extent, previously held convictions, but none so much as the 'risking' exhortation. For the older we get, the more conservative we become, until finally we are "too old to take chances" and proceed to park our lives in a garage, lock the doors and throw away the keys.

The book you're about to read will do everything possible to break down those doors, rev up your engine, slip a Count Basie disc in your player and point you towards the open road.

Instead of remaining hunkered down in a velvet-lined rut, you'll be urged to open your mind and arms to the unknown and untried. This is good medicine for what ails so many on the far side of fifty. The prescription includes a good dose of spiritual inspiration; an amalgam of Eastern philosophy, Western scriptures and Aquarian values. So as the five senses cease to entertain you, spiritual wings will find room to unfold, lifting the consciousness above physical aches and pains to a wonderful place that costs nothing to enter and remains open when all else is closed.

This transition is not necessarily an event scheduled for your fifties. Much of what you will read here is a preview of experiences and emotions to be encountered later in life.

The fifties, per se, aren't the problem. When most people reach this point of their lives, they're at the top of the hill, the high point of their lives. After all that climbing, the rest of the way looks easy. Ah, but rough terrain always appears smooth from high above. And verily, a few years down the road you'll come to some unmarked turns pitted with potholes. Now is the time to remove the blinders and practice evasive tactics. *As go your fifties, so goes the rest of your life.*

—H. Samm Coombs
Mill Valley, California

CHAPTER I

AGING IN A NEW AGE

You Couldn't Have Picked a Better Time To Be Fiftysomething.

What goes around comes around. Suddenly, *youth is uncouth* and *age is the rage!* Did you ever think you'd live to see this day?

Of course nothing happens suddenly in the demographic sphere. This shift from young to old was two decades in the making. But now that it's here, we are quick to contrast it to the last epoch's high water mark when Flower Children wagged our culture.

Remember? Anyone past '30' was beyond recall; not to be trusted.

How could you forget—after all, you were there, or somewhere close to there, in the face of The Establishment.

Now you are here, part of The Establishment, starting across that great divide separating middle-age from old-age.

And right on your heels march 78-million other Boomers, cutting their usual wide swath through the landscape; cocky as only a majority can be.

If you already are into your fifties you may be forgiven if you're just a touch resentful of all the attention paid those Johnny-Come-Lately Boomers. Anyone born before the Great Global War's denouement has, in the metaphor of football, spent their grown-up years running interference for those ball-hogging show-offs. They always got the cheers while you collected the lumps. Among the barriers you knocked down for them is the perception that '50' is old. You have lobbied to relabel this life cycle "middle age," making it a whole lot easier for those behind you to face their fifties. (There will come a time when the average life expectancy is, actually, 100 years. But in the meantime, calling the 50s *middle*-age must by considered an audacious act of affirmative thinking ... or, just plain chutzpah.)

But not to quibble about labels. They're just handles for columnists and commentators to grab onto.

If the fifties don't mark the middle of your life, they most certainly represent an in-between time. In that vein, the fifties might better be called 'the sandwich years.' Unappetizing? Okay, how about 'the threshold years?' That is both descriptive and sanitary—i.e., neatly avoids any reference to 'old' (which any book about this period had best avoid to have any hope of being read by those involved).

Nomenclature notwithstanding, your timing is perfect.

Wave maker

Those who will turn fifty in the next few years were born on the right side of WWII ... when the killing was about over and the procreating was about to begin. All

4

those babies have been making waves with each passing age, with you on the leading edge.

Your parents smeared those messy suburbs all over the map; put two cars (one of them a station wagon) in every garage, a Bar-B-Q on every patio. To give you an education the country had to reinvent the public school system. And when you graduated, your present was Vietnam, a rerun of Custer's Last Stand. Many of those who stood are no longer standing. Those who sought refuge in the Halls Of Ivy came back to fight another day with those who survived. While the graybeards who created the mess hid behind the power structure wagging their fingers.

No more of that. The Youth Movement cum Cultural Revolution that started in the wake of Kennedy, ended when Reagan's backside rode off into the sunset.

Some may wish it were otherwise. But there's no avoiding the demographer's curve. The future is silver.

And you are in its vanguard.

An irresistible force

Today, some 28-million of your fellow Americans are fiftysomething and counting. Every minute another one joins your parade. The rumble you hear behind you is a queue 50-million long waiting to fall in step behind you.

By the year 2025 those 78-million soulmates will have filled the 50-plus pool with 113-million men and women. Overseas they're aging even faster, with Japan and England leading the way.

The power of numbers

Already you control more than half this country's discretionary income and almost 80% of its assets.

With leverage like that who needs hair!

These numbers haven't been lost on marketers, much less politicians. Instead of illustrating callow kids in ads, now we're getting impossibly handsome, bronzed couples in golf carts with perfect smiles and lacquered coifs in settings as unreal as their persons. (Somebody save us from these cute seniors.)

Leery legislators, ever responsive to voting blocks, are beating the bushes surrounding America's ubiquitous retirement enclaves and continuing care communities where 86% of the inmates are registered to vote and 74% do. The politicos' solicitous sorties already have created a Federal trough overflowing with enticing entitlements. Deals dangle from every orange tree. Airlines, hotels, restaurants, theme parks, fast food franchises, *et alia*, woo you with senior subsidies and discounts. Every toilet has handrails and pity the poor transit system without wheel chair access (the cost of which is making public transit beyond the means of full-fare passengers!).

Already book shelves are filled with handbooks sourcing these perquisites. Racks of free guides show you the shortest distance to the dispensing agencies and bureaus.

Your unfair share
Many would say the elderly are getting more than their fair share. But these are voices in the wilderness; no match for organizations like the Grey Panthers and AARP.

And look who's doing the organizing: the very same group who reorganized America's social agenda in the 1960s. Antiauthoritarian and anything but conservative.

All things considered, this is a wonderful time to be fiftysomething.

Not that you don't deserve these desserts. The rest of the world has been giving elders their due for years now. In Japan they even have their own national holiday!

Putting experience back to work
Those who land on the plus side of fifty without a golden parachute will find more and more employers' doors wide open to their assembled experience. Indeed, by 2010 older Americans will comprise 25% of the work force (versus less than 10% today). Employers aren't becoming more magnanimous, exactly. They really have no choice in the matter. There just aren't enough people under 50 who can do what needs be done. You represent not only the most literate, skilled and available labor pool but the most responsible and, surprisingly, the least costly in terms of health care, absenteeism, and all the other indicia of 'valuable.' And who is better able to design and market products and services aimed at the fifty-plus crowd than men and women who have been there? A 29-year

old stock broker hasn't a clue when it comes to relating to a 60-year old investor's anxieties. Even advertising agencies, where pimples earn a premium, are augmenting their creative ranks with 'over the hill' taskforces. Patently, it takes a mouthful of false teeth to sell denture cement. Conclusion: As the 50+ market grows larger and larger, so will 50+ employment opportunities. But not before more than a few of you have been unceremoniously dumped in the name of 'down-sizing' (or 'right-sizing' as employers prefer to call it), a '90s phenomenon that's revisited in the next chapter.

Information junkies

Not surprisingly, media mavens are in the welcoming committee eagerly awaiting the Aging Of America, with publishers in the forefront. After all, someone fiftysomething is much more likely to consider thoughtful ideas on a printed page. You buy 6 out of every 10 books sold in this country. Periodicals that pander to your pains and passions are elbowing youth oriented rags off the stands with the same insouciance displayed by SEVENTEEN and ROLLING STONE when they buried SATURDAY EVENING POST and LIFE. First there was AARP's treacle-laced MODERN MATURITY, a compendium of institutional wisdom ladened with Shangri La-style images of 'active,' 'vital' and 'involved' seniors pursuing their lost youth in V-6 powered golf carts. The American Legion weighed in with LONGEVITY. And Reader's Digest, always quick to draw a bead on any disenfranchised reader, has unveiled NEW CHOICES, a retread of 50-PLUS (which debuted a couple of years before its time). While the mature woman has MIRABELLE to look out for her, aging males have to go it alone. Not that publishers are adverse to catering to older men, but it's been their experience that older men are less likely to read about their 'change of life' than are women. For one reason, menopause is a dramatic, not-to-be-denied metamorphosis. Whereas the change men experience is more subtle and easier to overlook (unless you are a young woman!). Along with these exclusionary monthlies, most of America's mainline mags are nodding to the mature niche with how-to and why-to articles on subjects dear to the hearts of anxious seniors.

Slick magazines are the least of it. Every day we loose another forest supplying newsprint to fill rusty newsstands with 'take-one' rags featuring 'Senior' somewhere on their mastheads.

Your love affair with the printed page has not dissuaded the electronic media from filling living rooms with wisecracking grandpas and blue-haired ladies on the make. And radio is not far behind. Ricky Nelson and peers have replaced Ol' Blue Eyes under the label, 'Golden Oldies'.

YOUNG PEOPLE ARE AN ENDANGERED SPECIES

Being surrounded by all this care and concern has its downside, of course. When you're in the majority, you become the cause of every problem and the butt of every joke. The higher the profile, the better the target. And you won't have young people to kick around anymore. The few specimens remaining will only rarely appear in public being too busy working overtime to keep you in your accustomed manner. (If you want a preview of 2025, visit Florida's Gold Coast. Even the nurses are over the hill.)

The 'New Age' cometh

There is another, much more sublime reason, outweighing all the others, for calling the 1990s the best of all possible times to be fiftysomething. All the portents bode well for this decade (beginning its third year, as every decade effectively does) to be the threshold of the lonnnng-awaited New Age, when finally and at last we've accumulated enough awareness of our relationship with the Divine to start a spiritual revival of the kind experienced 2000 years ago, albeit with a bit less acrimony, it is fervently hoped.

Spotting a trend-in-the making, much less an epoch, is an iffy business at best. And the point at which a rolling snowball becomes an avalanche may be moot to those who stand in its path. But certified futurists such as John Naisbitt and Wavy Gravy all agree on this one.

As the collective consciousness is raised exponentially, the Golden Rule will overcome old paradigms and inundate humankind in a landslide of love and connectedness, the hallmark of the Aquarian Age.

THE NEW AGE IS NOTHING NEW

The 'New Age' first debuted as such in the 1890s and reached cult proportions in the first decade of the 20th Century. Its first advocates were Edward Carpenter and Dr. R.M. Bucke, Whitman, Thomas Troward, Gurdjieff, Ouspensky, and yogi messengers such as Yogananda and Swami Abhedananda. The high hopes of those avatars were summarily smashed by two World Wars, when the forces of evil took command of the minds of men.

The approach of a new century always provides a springboard for new thought; a Millennium much more so. It has nothing to do with the calendar, per se, but the affect these milestones have on the public mind. People are more receptive to new ideas; more willing to discard the old and 'change the guard' when a new set of numbers mark the calendar.

The upcoming centenary is no exception. It will be even more so, given the momentous nature of this change over. There has been noth

(continued on page 11...)

Signs of Aquarius rising can already be seen in the quest for self-knowledge and an emerging global awareness that eventually will erase the divisiveness of gender, race and national distinctions. No, this spiritual awakening is far from complete. We have only one eye open.

(*continued from page 10*) ing like it since 999 became 1,000 (and little is known about that New Year, given the darkness that enveloped those times). The world awaits the coming of 2,000 A.D. with great expectations. When much is expected, much is accomplished. You'll see ...

There will be many bends in the road before The Consciousness Millennium is reached. The bad old 'me-against-them' days still loom large in our rear-view mirror. But the people who walk backwards into the future are no longer in control.

Those who have seen The Light up ahead are now in the driver's seat.

Ram Dass knows, and Ram Dass says, "If you liked the 60s, you're going to love the 90s."

The connection between then and now is you and your offspring. The flowers you planted in those halcyon times seeded the generation now about to bloom. ('X' marks their spot!)

A glorious Spring always is preceded by a long, cold winter of discontent, of the kind experienced in the 80s.

While the global garden was being ravaged by greedy reapers, New Age principals were germinating beneath their hobnail boots. Once they take root in the capitols of the world, it's Hallelujah time.

If history validates this point of view, those who reach fiftysomething during this changeover will be especially blessed. For just when your consciousness needs a lift crossing that great divide separating middle-age from old-age, along comes this breath of fresh air to give your spirit wings.

In times past, when spiritual values had no place in the material world, it was more difficult for the mind to rise above the snares and delusions of aging. Many of those who made it to their 60s and 70s arrived so disheartened, they just wanted to curl up and die. And many did.

The predicted paradigm shift will help your generation avoid that fate.

The Right Attitude

The luck of the draw has dealt you these advantages going in. But what you do with your senior years will have nothing to do with luck and everything to do with attitude, and values. These can be the most confining and monochromatic years of your life. Or the most expansive and colorful. It all depends on the posture you adopt in your 50s. This will be your stance for the rest of the dance; whether you do-si-do until the band stops playing or sit on your hands in the back of the hall sucking your teeth.

AGING IN A NEW AGE

NOTES TO MYSELF

CHAPTER II

FINDING YOURSELF IN THE LOST DECADE

Come Out, Come Out, Wherever You Are?

If the fiftysomething years are so well represented in the latest census tracts, how come no one's there to meet and greet you when you arrive? Not only are welcoming delegations missing, nobody waves good-bye when you depart for your sixties.

That's because no one's home on the fifties block. Everyone's someplace else, pretending they're '39' and holding. So there's no 'there' there. No signs point the way to the 'frantic fifties.' No bulletin boards explain what's doing there. There are no facilitators or coordinators; no mentors or mediators.

Your forties were not like that (with all the fuss'n'feathers about the infamous 'mid-life' crisis), nor will your sixties be like that (when you receive the first rites of senior citizendom).

The fiftysomething years are aptly acknowledged to be 'The Lost Decade,' the period psychologists forgot to study. Boston College sociologist David Karp calls the fifties "the most neglected" and least understood decade of the life cycle.

The sandwich years

One reason for this conspiracy of silence is that fiftysomething people are betwixt and between: beyond middle age but not yet aged. You are in the midst of *becoming* old and either you don't know it or won't admit it. It is hardly surprising you wish to relate to the period just passed rather than the one upcoming. (Whereas those on the flipside of the fifties—adolescents—ignore the past, spending their dreamtime in the future.)

This in-between position places you in a kind of void or vacuum, a limbo somewhere in the middle of nowhere. It amounts to a conspiracy of silence. Fiftysomething people don't cause a lot of trouble, or ask for a lot of help. Your wheels don't squeak. No one is waving a red flag or pounding on government gates on your behalf. Thus Uncle Sam isn't mindful of your status, and researchers don't find you terribly interesting.

Compared to other age groups, the 50 to 60 crowd has fewer of the social and economic problems that attract advocates and government programs.

The placid exterior shown by recent generations of fiftysomethings, combined with their small number, have rendered them inconspicuous. But all that is changing —faster than you can say "Baby Boomers." When they march into their fifties, shoulder to shoulder, bolder and bolder, in regimental pomp, beneath banners proclaiming their power and glory, you can bet they'll not tread lightly through this life cycle.

When this changing of the guard takes place, starting 1996, the fiftysomething years will no longer be 'lost' or 'neglected.' There will be research grants, tenured university chairs, congressional subcommittees, books about the books, programs and pressure groups, with experts of every stripe offering unsolicited opinions about this formerly misunderstood life cycle.

All that will be for the better.

There is no denying that the fifties represent a critical and traumatic passage. This is when most of us become aware we're no longer middle aged with half a life left to live. This realization usually comes suddenly and unceremoniously. The fifties place you on the edge of 'old' totally unprepared for what follows. A NEWSWEEK writer put it this way: "The shock of growing old is not that it happens; it's that it happens before we are ready." *We loose our younger self before we're able to piece together a new older self.* Such a self-identity vacuum can be most disconcerting, or something

THE PASSING OF 'THE SILENT GENERATION'

Until the 1990s came along, fiftysomething people were few and far between, being a product of the Great Depression when America had other things on its mind.

Those who reached fifty between the late 1970s and the early 1990s not only were few in number but belonged to the 'Silent Generation' or the 'tweeners' as humorist Roy Blount Jr. has labelled them. Born in the gloom and doom days preceeding the Great Global War, they came of age too late to be WWII heros, and too early to be Peaceniks. As Depression-era children and postwar collegians, they spent their adult life wedged between the GI Generation and those ubiquitous Boomers. At the age of consent they were smothered by the stultifying conformism of the 1950s then spent the rest of their lives making complex a world they found oversimple. Theirs has been the kindest generation of the 20th Century, flexible, caring and tolerant. Despite or because of these traits, they have been the first generation never to produce a president. Dating back to '69 they've been 0 for 6 in runs for the White House.

worse. The estimable Polly Francis is in agreement: "Age creeps up so stealthily that it is often with a shock that we become aware of its presence. Perhaps that is why so many of us reach old age utterly unprepared to meet its demands." To which the late M.K. Fisher added, "Parts of the aging process are scary, of course, but the more we know about them, the less they need be." For more on this subject listen to Daniel Levinson, Yale University emeritus professor of psychology who pioneered the adult life cycle study. "The early fifties are a time when you look at your life and try to modify it. We see what we can keep and how we can change." Professor Karp calls this period the "fulcrum years. If you don't leave your fifties with a good fix on how you want the rest of your life to be, almost certainly it will turn out to be something else." If ever there was a time to take charge of your life *it is now.*

And now for something completely different
Hereafter nothing's ever the same. You won't have the same marriage even though you're married to the same person. Life has changed for both parties.

Men tend to become more cautious and conservative with advancing age. Having labored long and hard, they are wont to protect their gains by holding their cards close to their vest (or beneath their mattresses), about which there's more to be said later.

Women, on the other hand, being no longer preoccupied with a nest full of fledglings, are inclined to want what has been denied them: a bit of freedom; a little excitement. Hubby is welcome to tag along if he's amind to. If not, she'll leave him to his couch and take off on her own. This contrariness, while societal in nature, places considerable stress on a marriage, causing many of those late-in-the-game divorces.

As more two-career couples come 'round the bend, this conflict may evaporate, leaving both parties crouched behind their moat ready to repel threats to their security.

Another change symptomatic of the fiftysomething years concerns work. Few people will have the same job in their fifties as before. Heretofore the changes have been voluntary. It's one thing to resign a corporate sinecure to grow organic raspberries for gourmet restaurants; to abandon a promising advertising career to join Greenpeace; to give up the law to enter a seminary, or to walk away from hard-won seniority in the airline mechanics union to import Mexican furniture. It's quite another thing to be summarily dismissed six months before your pension plan is fully vested; to find yourself on the short-end of a merger or a castoff from a leveraged buy-out. There is no security in competence; no reward for loyalty; no assurance your skills or expertise will remain in demand. For every golden parachute you see supporting a self-satisfied CEO, there are hundreds of free-falling bodies trailing screams of indignation. A Masters degree or 20 years of faithful service are no support. No one, it seems, is immune to the downside of downsizing, or the economic upheaval attending the end of the Cold War.

It is poetic justice that Boomers, having made it exceedingly difficult for Generation X to get started up the ladder, are finding the top rungs no longer will support the style they have become accustomed to.

Survival of the fittest

Resourcefulness, self-reliance, resilience and a hard-headed optimism (along with Universal Health Insurance) are the qualities you'll need to survive these uncertain economic times. The guarantees that secured the retirement of past generations no longer can be relied on. To stay afloat in the times ahead, you'll need to leave your stateroom on the promenade deck and take-over the helm. To gain headway, you'll need to jettison much of the luggage that accompanied you through your thirties and forties.

Along with realigning skills and allegiances, you'll need a change of consciousness.

At fiftysomething, some of those changes happen more or less automatically. For one thing, *you no longer think of your life in terms of how long you've lived but how much time you have left.* On the epidemiological level, you may enter your fifties feeling strong, but studies show there are preconditions programmed into our genetic codes that begin to manifest themselves in the fifties. High blood pressure, for example. Coinciding with this is a tendency to be "socialized into illness." When we enter our fifties, the culture teaches us to see ourselves more and more as patients. Instead of being as young as you feel, you're as old as other people make you feel. You playback society's perceptions ... unless you have a good self-image and understanding of where you fit in the cosmic scheme of things.

CHAPTER III

TIME HAPPENS

We Know From the Very Beginning There Will Be An End. But Don't Let That Bother You.

Timelessness is a state of being reserved for the primordial, all-generating spirit Christians like to call God. It also is a state of mind enjoyed by the very young, the insane, and those few realized beings who have attained Cosmic Consciousness·

For the rest of us, time is a tyrant that nips at our heels every step of life's journey. It is the Promethean paradox; the essential enigma.

It is convenient to consider time a man-made invention to account for our limited two-dimensional vision. Time measures movement, and movement requires the presence of a body in space. As long as our consciousness is housed in a body, we cannot be everywhere at the same time. God, being omnipresent, has no such problem. Being indivisible, the all-producing creative substance fills all space (*is* space), eliminating the need of time and place.

God's creations, when bound by form, can only function in the time/space continuum. This distorts our reality to say the least. We cannot see the trees for the forest. We are the forest but limit ourselves to being trees. Mumbo jumbo? If you say so.

"Without space there can be no time. When the elements of time and space are eliminated, all our ideas of things must necessarily be as subsisting in a universal here and an everlasting now."
—Thomas Troward

"There is no distance. Space is a fake idea belonging to separation. Day and night are the inflow and outflow from an ocean of everpresent time. All time is the present. Cease to hurry."
—*Christ In You*, Watkins

But you will have to agree that in our role as objects we know from experience there is a *now*. And we can recall a time before the present time which we take to be past time. This leads to the conclusion there is time not yet to be experienced or future time.

The biological process we call aging is measured by this linear scale. Longer relates to older; shorter to younger. The point of reference is you.

One of homo sapiens's defining qualities is our ability to distinguish between 'I' and the world. This gives us the capacity to keep time, which requires standing outside the present and imagining oneself back in the past or ahead in the future. This defining quality is the basis for man's most transcendent achievements: he can stand outside his history and thereby influence his own development (and, to a lessor extent influence the development of the society around him). But, of course, every plus comes with a complimentary minus. The price we pay for our ability to be self-conscious is anxiety; the fearful prospect of being alone and powerless.

Being able to stand outside time, to regulate the future based on the past, produces inward crises involving anguish and confusion. It is the breeding ground of regrets and resentments, and more times than not conspires to foul-up the present.

Being here now with the birds & bees

There is no indication other life forms operate on the same past/present/future continuum, at least in a manner that alters their mood and behavior. On the face of it, this is no boon. Anticipation is our cross to bear. For it means we know from the start there is an end, on the material plane. This is sound science. Physiologically, the dying process begins at the moment of birth.

Innocence would seem to be the more blissful state. Fishes do not worry about baited hooks or hungry pelicans patrolling overhead despite a lifetime of observing the fate of their finny fellows. The ant does not live in fear a boot may squash out its lights. Most of God's creatures spend their lives in an endless series of NOWs ... until the very last NOW.

How we handle the certainty of our biological end varies with our age. As our time draws closer, we are inclined to escape into the past. Remembering replaces anticipating, exactly the opposite from the days of our youth. That may be understandable, but it ain't no way to make the most of the present.

The trick, of course, is to remain in the Here & Now—the past being gone and the future being problematic. Easier said than done when you lost all your money yesterday and tomorrow the mortgage must be paid.

Tricky as it may be, there is a way to make the most of each and every moment/day without forgetting the past or denying the future. We'll get to that... in time.

But right now let's deal with more mundane matters. Like your age.

TIME HAPPENS

NOTES TO MYSELF

CHAPTER IV

HOW OLD IS OLD?

It Takes One a Long Time To Be Young.

—Picasso

You will not find here any numerical definition assigned to oldness. To each his/her own. There will come a time, in the foreseeable future, when this is not an all-important, life-and-death matter. Already 'old' is no longer old in the ways we used to mean. "People act 'youthful' according to their own expectations, and age has lost its meaning as a predictor of stamina and physiological health" says Bernice Neugarten who advocates an "age-irrelevant society." We are used to 28-year old mayors, 50-year old retirees, and 65-year old students. But the degree of irrelevance still is relatively irrelevant. Society's 'fitness' criteria continues to be based on 'appearances.'

The passage of time on the linear or quantitative scale obviously affects our materialized form. In time, these biological changes make us look different, feel different and act different.

First, and most noticeable, are changes wrought in our exterior packaging. Between the ages of, say, forty-five and sixty-five, those kind of changes are mostly superficial. That is, they don't cause us to act or feel different. Oh, sure, you may have lost a step in tennis;

your reactions may not be those of a 18-year old; but the differences in performance are relatively insignificant. The changes in your appearance, however, will cause others to treat you differently. A society of blind people presumably would not be segregated by age.

While there is more to be said on this subject of 'appearances' later, one other example will suffice for now. In many professions, age is a premium—it adds to your credibility and authority, as well as what you might charge for your services. It is entirely conceivable that a 29-year old neurosurgeon is every bit as competent as a 49-year old counterpart. But if it's *your* head that's being operated on, wouldn't you feel more confident looking up and seeing a graybeard wielding the laser? If it were an emergency procedure so you didn't meet the surgeon prior to the operation, the whole question would be a non question. Wherever you look, its the same story, though often as not the roles are reversed. Were a 65-year old ad man to present an inspired campaign theme for Levis, it would be rejected out of hand as being hopelessly outdated; lacking the right spirit; whatever. (In actual fact, of the few 65-year old admen and women still extant, none would ever be invited to make such a presentation!) But if that same inspiration were represented as coming from a younger person, it would be allowed to seek its proper level. This is no big surprise. Age prejudice, whether for or against the elderly, is based not on performance as much as appearance; changes in your external packaging.

HOW OLD IS OLD?

America the youthful

The United States Of America has always been a youth-oriented society. This is about to change, but the changeover will not be without considerable stress and strain among those about to turn fifty; they being the generation most obsessed with youth.

In fairness, this fixation has been a long time in the making, going back to the Revolution which was the work of young men; as was the Constitution. It was young men and women who took Horace Greely's advice and went West (where the average age of state and territorial legislatures was in the early 30s).

This history has produced a national attitude and value system that considers youth to be the norm, and anything else less than worthwhile or inferior. As a consequence, America's older population suffers from an inferiority complex: They're apologetic; *embarrassed to be old.* Feeling unwanted and unneeded, elders tend to gather in flocks —like birds of a feather— creating a clan-like mentality that breeds a numbing self-absorption.

Apartheid

Everything about our society promotes this separation. There's no room in today's condos for grandma. And even if there were, there's no one home during the day to make sure she takes her medicine.

Being set apart creates an adversarial attitude that is

making seniors a selfish and spoiled 'special interest' group who skillfully use their growing numbers to keep their trough filled with freebies, special dispensations, and perquisites, all at the expense of a shrinking working class. Such is the price of segregation.

New versus old

The New World's attitude toward age is in sharp contrast to the Old World, including the Third World. There the aged are respected and in some cases venerated for their accumulated experience (the raw material of wisdom).

In primitive cultures, as well as in some advanced societies such as Japan, old age is a privileged status that is anticipated with pleasure. The elders are the custodians of the clan or nation's memories, the story-tellers, sages and shamans.

The sparks that flew in the 60s and 70s were to some extent caused by old leaders rubbing up against a youthful, 'now' minded population. Remember? You were there! And now look where you are: Fiftysomething and counting. And you're about to be joined by 78-million others. It remains to be seen if you'll use your majority to install leaders as old as yourselves, or you'll remember what it was to be young and unrepresented. One would be ironic; the other poetic.

Whether or not we grow old in a hostile or friendly environment, one thing's for sure: once there, there's no turning back.

HOW OLD IS OLD?

All else is not (always) equal

Some of us jog into the autumn of our years maintaining a sunny disposition every step of the way. Others loose their leaves and wither out of season.

How time affects our bodies depends largely on the genes we are dealt, and how we care for our inheritance over the years. Attitude certainly can alter the outcome, as you will read. But our attitudes also are affected by the passing of time. Young, inexperienced people usually have a devil-may-care attitude. While the village elders' cautious outlook reflect a knowledge of what can go wrong.

Consciousness doesn't age

You literally are not the same person you were seven years ago. Every single cell in your body has changed in that time. Indeed, within the space of seven years every part of you—your brain, your heart, your blood, your fingers—is renewed; a process that slows with advancing age until that rejuvenation process ceases altogether—i.e., when the making of 'new' cells slows to the point that the 'old' cells begin to dominate. If it's any consolation, at fiftysomething your 'cell factory' is still cranking out shiny new parts—albeit not as rapidly as before—so that nothing remains of the old you except your 'I Am'; the witnessing part of you that remains aware of the changes. You have retained the same sense of 'I' since childhood. This is the part of you that is birthless and deathless. It is the persistent, changeless you; that which remains whole while parts of your physical form become diseased and are removed.

Like electromagnetic energy, the consciousness lacks mass, so there's nothing to deteriorate; nothing to age.

Some may be more comfortable calling this essence the soul or spirit. Whatever it is, it's of much more consequence than that which gives it form. However, as the subject of this discussion is linear time and the effect that has on the you that others see, consider how we react when confronted with the visible evidence of aging.

You can look forward to being 'old' much longer than you were 'young' or even 'middle-aged.' You were a baby for a brief 3 years, while your childhood only lasted 10 years, from 3 to 13. Adolescence was a short 5 years with youth extending from there to your early 30's, after which (by definition) comes middle-age, the span of which has recently been extended well into the 50's. Following that comes the various stages of old: young old, frail old and old old.

With longevity increasing at its present alarming rate you are liable to be labeled 'old' for thirty or more years; more than any of the preceding life cycles. Therefore it seems the better part of wisdom to get comfortable in this new role.

The moment of truth

We begin to age at the moment of birth. But the aging we're concerned with begins in our thirties. The changes are slow and subtle, to begin with. But sooner or later the ravages of time become obvious even to someone who sees us every day, like ourselves! While the process is gradual, there is nothing gradual about its recognition. It comes in a moment ... a moment of truth!

It might be triggered by an unexpected glimpse of yourself when passing a mirror. That person looks like your mother or father looked when you thought they looked old. Or a bunch of photos come back from the developers. M'gawd, that's me?! That's you!

If your self-esteem is largely dependent on Springtime beauty and potency, you are a candidate for depression.

Appearances are deceiving

Nothing prepared you for this confrontation. You had always assumed you'd feel old when you looked old. Nobody ever told you you'd feel '30' approaching '60.' Appearances really are deceiving.

Now a whole series of disquieting realizations come rushing to the fore. People who are fiftysomething find all the dimbulbs they grew up with are now in charge! The klutz who spent two years getting out of 5th Grade is now operating on people's heads at the Mayo clinic! That crazy kid who played with fire is in command of an underground Minuteman missile silo somewhere in North Dakota. The responsible grown-ups you always had depended

GILDING THE TOTAL

Sometime after '39' and before '70' we are inclined to shave a few years off our age if someone is so impertinent to ask. (It's usually some functionary with a form to fill out, although there are quite a few bratty, precocious children out there who are not the least hesitant to confront you with the question if only to see you squirm.)

Men are motivated to take the edge off the truth for reasons of romance, or when their livelihood is at risk.

Women are not so particular. For obvious reasons, all cultural, women have no compunction about telling a bald-faced lie, figuring, no doubt, anyone so rude to ask so crude a question deserves no better. Often the answer is calculated to beg the question. "Old enough to know better, young enough not to give a damn." Or, a 54-year old might reply, "Let's say I'm closer to 50 than to 40."

After '70' a reverse reaction takes place. Subterfuge is abandoned for the pride of endurance. Indeed, those who have persisted eight, nine and ten decades are anxious to share their longevity with anyone who'll listen. How often have you heard

(continued on page 36...)

(continued from page 35...)
some old fogey ask a perfect stranger, "How old do you think I am, eh?" The response invariably will be safely off the mark allowing the octogenarian to proudly retort, "Naw, you're 'way short, sonny."

on are now you and your friends. A sobering reality.

Look who's in charge

As you approach sixty it only gets worse. Authorities like policemen and firemen, the Mayor, judges, jailers are your nieces and nephews. People in charge of your welfare don't even know what you know, f'Godssake.

After looking up to your elders all those years, now you're up there looking down. That view makes it hard to reconcile the attainments of younger men and women, among other things. You have been explaining your position in life, consciously or not, relative to your age. So what if you weren't yet a Vice President or the author of The Great American Novel. What can you expect of someone so young (as you once were)? Somewhere back there you had lost that youthful prerogative that allows you to accomplish not much of anything except exude potential. Your *enfant terrible* period is past. No longer are you allowed to speak in unfinished sentences and show up for work late. You are without all those youthful 'excuses.'

All your (past) life you were full of becoming. You had all those expectations and options. Now you have crossed, unnoticed, your Rubicon and now find yourself confronted with limitations—things you can no longer do or be. So maybe you never wanted to be an astronaut, a Playboy bunny, an Olympic hurdler, a 747 Captain, a millionaire before 40, a fireman, the youngest President, a mother of seven. But those possibilities were reassuring; the stuff of which daydreams are made. As soon as we're denied something, its value increases. (Conversely, we devalue that which has been attained.)

"(At fiftysomething) I had grown too old ever to die young."
—Meg Greenfield

Now or never.

This sudden confluence of 'cannots' causes some of us to go into a blue funk and remain there. Others become manic. It's *now-or-never* time; a time for making changes: in mates, careers, geography, you name it. Time is running out.

Sensing you are about to be stuck with your past, you resolve to rewrite the script; add some episodes worth remembering.

But first you've got to be rid of the past.

CHAPTER V

HANDLING THE PAST

Required Reading for "Tragedy Queens' and Other Cry Babies

We accumulate a lot of excess baggage on our journey through life: fears, phobias, quirks, anxieties, and a closet-full of might-have-beens. Whatever your present attainments, they're not likely to be what you wanted, or expected, or what you're capable of, and satisfied with.

We aren't hesitant to blame the present state of our affairs on forces beyond our control. Spouses are a favorite target, with employers and parents next in line. Government (usually in the form of a certain agency like FEMA, the police, the postal service, the local unemployment bureau or the dastardly IRS) makes a handy whipping boy, along with multinational corporations, lawyers and the Pope. (No more Communists!)

This propensity to blame others not only eliminates any chance to learn from the past; it infects our consciousness with *resentments;* an ailment from which there is no recovery ... except by taking responsibility.

Keep your hands on the wheel.

You can't fix what you don't control. When you conclude the cause for your discontent lies outside yourself,
you are agreeing to remain discontented forevermore.
You have declared yourself helpless and hopeless. Not
only did you not get what you wanted, you gained an
enemy after the fact, and agreed to become a permanent
victim. That makes you a 3-time loser!

The wiser course is to accept responsibility for whatever comes your way—whether or not you can see any
connection between your thoughts and actions and the
resented result. For in truth *nothing good nor bad can happen
to you without your agreement,* however tacit and unconscious.

Forgotten causes; remembered effects.

To be sure, sometimes it isn't so clear where you went
'wrong.' A lot of un-good things happen that don't appear traceable to any act or attitude on your part. Well,
too often that's your ego's defense mechanism working
to protect itself. Most times, if you hunt hard enough,
you'll discover you created the cause that produced the
effect—however delayed it was in manifesting itself.

The Hindus explain tragedy—ill fate that befalls the
seemingly innocent—as a harvesting of acts committed
in a previous existence: your Karma. But most often you
won't have to go back that far. Maybe beyond last week.
Maybe as far back as your childhood. But somewhere
back there you planted the seed that produced today's
bitter harvest.

That's how the universe works, with perfect consistency.

That's the only way it can work. If a cause produced no effect or an action produced no reaction, the cosmos would self-destruct. The fact that it hasn't indicates everything is in perfect working order. Maybe the timetable is not to your liking. That's your decision, and your responsibility. Don't expect the planets to alter their orbits to accommodate your allusions.

Again, effects don't always have an identifiable cause, but that doesn't mean there isn't one. It just means you can't or won't comprehend it. In that case accept it. When something goes amiss, accept at face value you are the cause of it. One: it's true. Two: you escape all those personally disturbing feelings when you lay the blame on your boss, Republicans, the Devil, the weather or the local gendarmerie.

Probably none of this comes as any big news. After fiftysomething years, you've learned a thing or two about life. Trouble is, we put into practice very little of what we learn. To make a practice of it, it must be made practical, as in 'applicable.' Here's an example of how this lesson can work on the street level.

Don't plead innocence

Let's say someone was heading home after a hard day at the office when all of a sudden this law-abiding citizen walks into the middle of a protest march that's attacked by club-swinging cops. In the melee this 'innocent' bystander is conked on the head. Certainly that person would be sympathized with if he declared himself a victim of unjust treatment.

But the universe doesn't assign labels like 'unjust' or 'innocent' to people and events. In order to be knocked on the noggin, he had to be in the vicinity of the noggin-knocking. That was his choice; a choice that involved risk. (Every choice does!) Even if he couldn't extract himself from the middle of the SWAT-Team offensive—he was, in fact, there. And there's where he should leave it. But most of us make matters worse by picking up the burden of resentment. His resentment of that cop carries over to all cops. One more monkey to carry around on his back. Who needs it? If he'd said, "Oops! I was there. It turned out to be the wrong place." Then the worst is over. His head was sore. He had been inconvenienced. But he wasn't crippled with resentment.

It isn't a question of fault; its a matter of responsibility. Taking responsibility won't turn you into a doormat. Nobody's recommending you roll over and play dead.

When Jesus advised, "Turn the other cheek ..." He wasn't being holier-than-thou. As usual, He was being terribly practical. To "suffer the slings and arrows of outrageous fortune" may be ennobling. To "set up arms against a sea of troubles" surely will cause worse troubles.

Cosmic justice

We humans cry out for justice; and it is there. The Greater Power we know as God metes out perfect justice. You don't have to play the judge. Trust the architect of the atom and the galaxies to treat you fairly. If you choose to head upstream without a paddle, don't blame the river for making it tough.

When you take personal responsibility for something you think turned out wrong, you are in a position to make it right. You can only do something about you. That's all you can do. That's all you need do. If each and every person cleaned up his or her own act, nobody would be messed up—it'd be Heaven On Earth. Hallelujah!

Jealousy and self-pity, like resentment, are cop-outs, ways to avoid the responsibility for running your own life.

Good luck

Taking responsibility has a plus side—it's not just a way of reconciling problems and removing resentments. Taking responsibility is also taking credit. When something good happens to you, it's no more good luck than bad things are bad luck. You are the cause of those good things. You deserve what you get. Even if you stumble onto buried treasure while chasing butterflies. You were there. You made it happen. Enjoy.

On the street of regret

Another piece of excess baggage you should discard instanter is regrets. We collect a lot of those (in the form of 'if onlys') along the way. While not as disabling as resentments, regrets waste a lot of precious time. By defi-

43

nition, regrets relate to the past, causing us to feel sad/bad/mad in the present. Every minute you feel that, is a minute you could be doing something to make you feel glad/good/happy. So in regretting some bygone event you allow it to pollute the present.

By the time some people turn fifty, accumulated regrets are running their lives. It is rather important, therefore, to get a handle on those past regrets and chuck them. And even more importantly, do not allow future disappointments to generate new regrets.

If only ...?

Unlike resentments, regrets follow the acknowledgment of our own miscues. "If only I hadn't asked for a divorce ...", "If only we had moved to California before Proposition 13 was in effect ..." "If only I had or hadn't said or done this or that ..." There are a number of false premises involved here. Had you done something differently who knows but what the result might have been even more horrendous. Or the consequence you regret now might yet prove be to your advantage, given the passage of more time. In reality, of course, those if-onlys are a figment of your imagination; a denial of reality. What is, *is*. What isn't, *isn't*.

Happiness, someone said, is accepting what-is when you can't change it. The key is not 'happiness' or 'what-is' but *accepting*. Insofar as there's no accepting what isn't; what other choice is there? There are no 'might have

beens,' no other possibilities are possible. Once an oc-
currence occurs, it could not have occurred any other
way, with any other result. But O' what a lot of time and
energy is wasted playing house with an illusionary past.

Life after fifty is enough to handle without dragging
along the deadweight of resentments and regrets. Let
loose of'em. It's as easy as that.

CHAPTER VI

FACING THE ABYSS

Living With Your Back to The Edge

Among the unsettling moments experienced in later life is the loss of one's parents. This happens most frequently when you're fiftysomething.

When the second parent disappears from your reality you are suddenly alone in a way you've never been 'alone' before, with no buffer between you and the ... abyss.

For the eldest offspring, this changing of the guard is all the more traumatic. No matter what your age when this event happens, the impact is the same.

No place to hide.

When the baton is passed to your hands, there is no refusing it. Nothing in fact has changed regarding your own mortality and life expectancy. It's strictly an emotional response. What was, heretofore, an intellectual reality is now a gut issue. You may be excused for feeling exposed, threatened, vulnerable, and terribly isolated. It's a mindless fright; a feeling that's difficult enough to explain to yourself much less anyone else. It never really goes away, you just learn to live with this nagging reality. Most of us contain this emotion by filing it in some accessible cubbyhole in our psyche where it won't interfere with the business of living.

Peter Pan's demise

Nothing's quite the same after both parents pass on. You are no more a child. There is no one to be happy or concerned about your victories and defeats the way parents are. You don't confide in and consult with your spouse or children the way you do with parents. No one feels towards you the way your parents do. All that is finished when you step into the vacancy created by their passing. Emotionally speaking it's a big step that moves you into the elders' tent, ready or not. Like it or not.

Changing the guard

This new role affects different people different ways. Most of us do what patriarchs do: become the point man (or woman) for the extended family. In this role we take a new-found interest in and responsibility for nieces and nephews and second cousins in law. Now you are the featured attraction at those family gatherings that once interfered with more important things. You become the librarian for all the inherited memorabilia and may feel called on to contribute some pages to the family's history, spoken or written.

Not only do you look at your relations differently; your relatives see you in a different perspective. The person who stands at the edge gains a degree of respect. Your foibles and shortcomings are more easily forgiven. You begin to receive seasonal notes and Sunday phone calls from distant cousins. You are consulted and listened to.

Everything's different,
but nothing's changed

When this metamorphosis occurs in your 50s, you need a firm grip on reality. While still a long way from your D-Day, your mortality has a higher profile now. The prospect of your demise has now taken up residence in your subconscious from whence it can emerge without warning to disturb your tranquility. It can fill your objective mind with doubts and indecision. "Why get a face lift?" "What's the point of taking up tennis?" "Who cares about long-term Capital Gains?" This feeling of pointlessness fades away, unless you become mesmerized by your mortality.

FOR PITY'S SAKE

As people pass their actuarial limits and start living on 'borrowed time,' some become so preoccupied with their mortality, they look for any excuse to remind friends and loved ones of their imminent departure.

We all know the type. A casual 'Howareyou?' greeting elicits a wistful, 'I can't complain, considering ...' This is by way of saying they are silently suffering the infirmities of old age (sigh) but don't wish to burden you with a list of their complaints (groan). When its time for good-byes, a simple 'Seeyoulater' inevitably elicits a pathetic, 'You may' (by way of reminding you that you may not!).

These people might just as well go round carrying a big 'I QUIT' sign. They're a burden to themselves and everyone who comes in contact with them.

Waiting to die is no way to live.

Fear of falling

Being on the edge is inhibiting. It's not easy to perform handsprings and cartwheels when one false move could be your last. The threat may be all in your head, but that can turn your feet to lead. The only way to carry-on as if nothing had changed is to turn around and face life, your back to the yawning abyss.

A legacy of love

If there is a tragedy to be found in this scenario, it is one of unfinished business. If the last parent to go is the father, there is a good chance (sorry to say), he departed without leaving a legacy of love. That is to say, he left an emotional vacuum, never having spoken of what was in his heart. Had he been asked by his offspring any time during his fatherhood, "Do you love me, father?" most likely he would have replied, "But of course I do, you are my son/daughter, after all. It goes without saying." But, of course, it doesn't go without saying. Actions do not always speak louder than words. There is no substitute for "I-love-you," when that is volunteered; inserted into the business of living, apropos of nothing in particular.

Too often the father's role, particularly in the American household, is that of the controller, the guardian; one who is not given to soppy emotion. That is left to mother. Thank Heaven she is usually up to the task. But the father who is unwilling or unable to acknowledge his feelings is less a father than a master. He may leave you with a feeling of respect and gratitude for his sacrifices and accomplishments, but these emotions don't complete the relationship; they don't leave you wrapped in a blanket of love that will permanently warm and reassure you.

To be sure, love is more than words. But acts of love are empty if they are never proceeded and ended with a declaration. Those three little words add much to a hug, a squeeze, a loving look. They complete the act.

To have lost a father who failed to complete his relationship in this way leaves you feeling incomplete, lacking your creator's stamp of approval. Children who are left to wonder how a parent *really* felt towards them will spend their lives as emotional orphans.

The love between parent and child is a force as basic as gravity. It is what the Creator feels towards His creations. It is not the freely chosen or selective love between man and woman. It is beyond loyalty or affiliation. Most importantly, it is not a conditional, upon-approval love that must be earned. It is a come-what-may, irrational, transcendent love that dissolves all barriers. It is a bonding of flesh and blood. You may not like what your children do, you may withhold your approval of their choice in clothes, music, friends, spouse. But these do not in any way diminish the bond of love that exists between parent and child.

This is mentioned not so much to sympathize with those who may have been left dangling in that emotional limbo, but to encourage fiftysomething parents to consider the emotional legacy you'll be leaving.

If there are children, and your relationship hasn't been cemented with frequent and voluntary expressions of your unconditional love, that should be corrected instanter. If such displays are inconsistent with your modus operandi,

--◄►--

MORE LOVE

For more on the magic of love, read, *If He Loves Me, Why Doesn't He Tell Me,* by Hal Larson.

--◄►--

then change your M.O., not by degrees, over time, but totally and immediately, giving new meaning to being 'born again.'

Love has a life of its own

Those three little words not only will change the nature of the relationship between you and your children, they will change each of you individually, and all for the better. And when you are separated in form, that bond will keep you together on a higher plane.

NOTES TO MYSELF

CHAPTER VII

WHERE TO TURN WHEN THE THRILL IS GONE

Developing Inner Resources To
Fill the Coming Vacuum

People who reach fiftysomething totally dependent on external gratification end up holding an empty bag. Those thrills don't last. All too suddenly life can be drained of meaning when you're no longer on stage starring in your former role as 747 Captain, tenured professor, Private Investigator, PTA president (or whatever you do). If your supply of internal self-esteem is insufficient to fill the empty space, angst and ennui will.

The sooner you face the fact there's no future in the physical, sense-oriented world, the sooner it can be replaced with something that will never let you down. Never.

As the body begins to fold, our spiritual wings should be given room to spread. If for no other reason than to rise above the physical compromises and psychic upheaval of aging. The transition from an earth-bound creature to Heaven-bound being will happen of its own volition if you just let go of your past and allow your consciousness to flow with the present.

This new state of mind does not require wealth or even good health. (Those are by-products.)

TIME HAPPENS

The beginners mind

All that's required is an open mind; what Eastern phi-
losophies call 'The Beginners Mind,' a state of mind open
to any possibility. Easy for children and primitive cultures. But after fiftysomething years relying on sight,
sound, touch, taste and smell, all kinds of mental static
interferes with your spiritual receptivity.

The transition is especially complicated for those
people who, at twentysomething, had their minds made
up about *everything*, and spent the intervening time prov-
ing themselves right. A lifelong Republican, Mormon,
Peorian, Rotarian is likely to have more difficulty adjust-
ing to old-age than those persons whose allegiances, sym-
pathies, habits and beliefs have been in constant flux.
Rather than stand accused of duplicity or lack of principals, those who voted for Nixon in '60 and McGovern in
'72 should be seen as open-minded and adaptable; better
able to accept the imposition of new conditions. Their
changes of heart come from an open, receptive mind. A
closed door might as well be a wall.

Dueling with duality.

Some minds close at an early age to avoid dealing
with dualities. In actual fact, what they wish to avoid is
questioning. Because every question has two sides to it.
When nothing is questioned, nothing is learned. Life
becomes one-sided, tilted, off-balance, a total bore. It
takes two to tango; two to argue; two to agree. A winner
requires a looser. Likewise, there can be no appreciation

56

of beauty without the presence of ugliness. Wealth requires poverty as Good does Evil. It seems everything comes in pairs. Yin & Yang rule the universe. Equilibrium requires equal opposites—i.e. opposition. Certainly this applies to what we call our mind.

Two minds

We are often 'of two minds' about this or that. One mind tells us what our ego or senses want to hear; the other 'higher' mind tells us what is morally right. The *sense mind* might urge you to engage in unsafe sex while your reflective mind whispers a caution in the background.

The subjective mind witnesses your ego's antics; commenting on your workaday activities. It is the voice you hear in a cathedral, and late at night when your ear is pressed to a pillow.

The objective mind 'speaks' with a social or conditional voice. It assesses the prevailing conditions before it talks, then chooses the politically-correct words; what it takes to persuade or impress a particular audience. The subjective mind monitors your performance, judging it according to your value system. In this sense, 'being objective' really means, being pragmatic, a so-called realist. We are seldom 'honest with ourselves' audibly. How many times have you allowed, out loud, you were acting like an ass—e or being hypocritical? That's a job for the subjective voice. (Of course, there are one-minded people who never hear from that side—their egos long ago rendered their subjective voice speechless.) How about you—have you ever heard your self saying something and subjectively criticized what you were saying as you were saying it? If so, there's hope.

YOU VERSUS 'THEM'

Because your consciousness is presently sheathed in a fleshy facade which occupies a different space than other objects, you consider your self to be separate and apart; alone and vulnerable. This produces a defensive posture in some people, while others turn aggressive.

Most everything we experience reinforces this illusion of separateness. The tree is not me so it's okay to chop it down. She is not me, so it's okay to hurt her. 'They' are not me so it's okay to hate 'them.' All the un-good feelings that come our way—shyness, inferiority, resentment, jealousy, ad nauseam—are fostered by this sense of being apart and alone in an alien universe. No wonder you feel oppressed, inadequate, threatened, scared, confused and want to run and hide.

The self-conscious ego is the part of you that's diminished when you lose a limb or some organ. The soldier who comes back from the wars in a wheelchair may feel like only half a man, but all he's lost are pieces of that fleshy fa-

(continued on page 59...)

These two minds often work in tandem, albeit not harmoniously. Your objective voice can be pontificating while your subjective mind, seeing the audience is getting restless, tells you to "get to the point."

The objective mind is temporal; an instrument of your senses; a tool of the body, the ego's voice. It is what identifies you, makes you *self*-conscious, separate and apart and often at odds with your fellow beings and the environment.

The objective mind, to be certain, is essential to your physical survival. It is used to gain an advantage, to dominate, coerce and manipulate. Whereas the subjective mind referees and judges. It deals with 'right' and 'wrong.' It is unlikely our beetle-browed ancestors were endowed with anything resembling morality. (Or they wouldn't have lasted very long.) As you will read, morality is a recently acquired faculty, still unevenly distributed amongst our kind.

A force to be reckoned with

The subjective mind can reinforce or supercharge the objective mind. Peak performance is attained when both are working together; the subjective motivating the objective.

This is what enables a 90-pound mother to lift a 2000-pound automobile if her child is under it. When all systems are in sync and focused, the effect is superhuman.

The voice of the ages

At this time of life, you would do well to amplify the subjective, for this is for the ages; being the voice of the consciousness that will accompany you for all eternity. This, also, is the domain of inspiration and intuition, a place of perfect bliss beyond pain and sorrow, where you are one with the cosmos. It is the same immortal stuff as the originating energy, the starting point of all matter, subsisting in every moment of all time, in the innermost nature of all being. Indeed, your subjective mind gives you the reins to the Universe.

The battle between the objective

(continued from page 58...)
cade. If he thinks that's all he is, he feels reduced. But his consciousness that went into battle and returned home with him hasn't been reduced. That's still whole. That's indivisible, indestructible, which is to say immortal.

APPEARANCES ARE DECEIVING

Because you are not what you appear to be —a separate body/ego apart from all other bodies/egos— but are in fact a part of a whole, everything that comprises that whole is interdependent, and not just in an ecological sense. As a great Hassidic rabbi once put it, "If I am I because you are you, and if you are you because I am I, then I am not I and you are not you."

and subjective mind lasts a lifetime. The outcome is never in doubt, however, as the subjective or spiritual mind, being indestructible, is destined to prevail. But the sooner the better. For the subjective mind provides a refuge from material want and physical hurt as well as a preview of things to come (when you no longer hear two voices).

Inner voices

Because the subjective voice is internalized, it is first heard but faintly. To raise the volume you must retreat from the ego's battlefield in order to quiet the objective or rational mind.

The Western world resists such suggestions. Shutting down the cerebral cortex (the thinking generator of the brain that manufacturers all our miseries) is related to going out of our minds. And that is where you must go to get to higher levels of truth—the ultimate reality.

There are many different routes to this end. For some it's via a church or a cult. Psychedelics will get you there, albeit a mite too fast (and at the risk of psychic shock). Meditation will take you there without any detours or dead ends. This method quiets all the voices that harass you in the material world. The meditative process also recharges your psychic batteries by plugging you into the cosmic power source.

When overloaded, the objective

LISTEN TO LAO-TSU

Stop talking, stop thinking and there is nothing you will not understand. Those who know, do not talk.

The quieter you become, the more you hear.

mind can put so much stress on the nervous system that if unrelieved may cause Nature's circuit breaker to switch off objective reality. Meditation or its technological parody, BioFeedback, serve to prevent nervous breakdowns.

The two realities

The objective and subjective minds are doors to two different realities, henceforth to be called, Reality I and II, respectively.

Reality I is the world of externalizations; the outer world ruled by the senses, the dominion of the objective mind. This reality comprises the 'cruel world' of gross, material objects, where times passes and good guys don't always finish first.

As long as we take our marching orders from our objective mind, we are limited by time and space and self-imposed secondary conditions.

If this is the only voice you listen to, you'll only hear one side of any question—the selfish, greedy, shortsighted side.

Reality II is the inner world where the spirit dwells in a continuous present. This level of reality is produced by a subjective consciousness that literally can rise above the body—i.e., exist without form.

Everyone operates within these two realities, although most of us only recognize one, Reality I, the bailiwick of our physical self where 'things' are seeable, touchable, hearable and smellable. When these perceptions rule, they effectively imprison our spiritual force.

Both realities are governed by laws, but we find it easier to obey the laws regulating objects than those that relate to thought. We can see the former. We require a laboratory to 'see' the latter. And anything we can't see, touch, feel or smell unaided, we're inclined to discount.

Reality I and II are not opposing camps. As revealed earlier, they can and do co-exist, with the latter aiding and abetting the former. A pretty good definition of a 'to-gether' person is one who keeps both realities in balance, working together synergistically. Those are the people with well-integrated personalities, who seem to "have everything going for them." It's as if they had an extra power source; two engines instead of one. Reality II makes Reality I work better. It isn't just somewhere to hide from the cruel, material world. Reality II helps sharpen the tools you use to dig with in Reality I. The idea is to apply Reality II *principles* to Reality I *practices*. "Doing unto others ..." is good both for business *and* the soul.

"Is that all there is?"
Your experience to-date no doubt has kept you on the Reality I stage.

APPEARANCES ARE DECEIVING (CONTINUED)

When speaking of material objects, whether rocks or bodies, we take them at face value as being solid, dense and opaque. The reality is quite different. Those 'solid' objects are made up of atoms that can be split into particles or electrons. These are more like clouds of electricity that orbit a nucleus. All 'solid' matter is like this. Were you take a man's body and squeeze all the empty spaces (between those atomic particles) out of him, what would be left would be no bigger than a flyspeck. We are, in effect, hollow; our insubstantial bodies held together with electromagnetic and nuclear forces, creating the illusion of solid matter.

But that show is coming to an end and the audience will move on to applaud other illusions, leaving you alone with Peggy Lee's plaintiff lyric echoing in your mind, "Is That All There Is?" No, indeed.

The world monitored by the five senses is predictable, being subject to understood physical laws. It also is 'cold,' as in 'scientific,' and seemingly cruel if left to its own devices. But our senses are limited. Our mind is not! It can release high frequency electromagnetic forces (in the Reality II spectrum) that can move or alter objects. This power is called willpower.

When you tune out the low frequencies that radiate from base (material) objects and tune-in the higher vibrational levels that emanate from the subjective or spiritual consciousness things get really interesting. In this reality the individual can transcend physical boundaries. Here you get to create your own reality. That's what makes it the ideal playground for the elderly.

CHAPTER VIII

THE PROBLEM WITH PROBLEMS

Nobody Promised You a Rose
Garden Without Thorns

There is another surprise awaiting you at fiftysomething. By this time of life, most people expect to be rid of the problems that hassled them in the past; no more worries at work, no more problems at home. Ho-ho, Hah-hah!

As it turns out, there's no end to those problems— no relief for the weary.

It would appear each of us has a certain carrying capacity for problems. You might have a 10-gallon capacity; someone else can handle only 3 quarts. Whatever it is, it's always filled. Get rid of one problem and another will rush in to fill the void. (Which might recommend hanging onto those old familiar problems rather than solving them only to be confronted with a whole new set that you'll have to 'break-in.')

This is not being cynical or pessimistic. Problems don't mean you can't enjoy life. They don't exclude a day in the park, sex, a good book, a bit of pastry, friends, a little wine and dignity. Problems aren't inherently bad. They are only bad if you handle them badly; allow them to affect you badly, to the point they interfere with sex, sunshine, *et alia*.

Avoiding the snowball effect

So it's kind of dumb to complain about problems. Rather it will better serve you to understand the nature of problems; knowledge that will prevent small problems from becoming bigger problems.

All problems are personal. And being personal, relative. Perhaps you've noticed that nobody has problems like *your* problems. It's the same for everybody else. To underscore the seriousness of *your* problems, you're quick to tell anybody who'll listen how happy you'd be to trade with them. People with physical problems would gladly exchange them for financial problems. The person with a 'problem' spouse would much rather have a 'problem' boss or neighbor, as poor people would gladly trade the problems of poverty for the problems produced by wealth. Kids would love to have a grown-up's problems, and vice versa.

Acne and bankruptcy

This willingness to trade problems leads to another rule. A small problem is a big problem when it's the only problem you have. Thus it's possible for a teenager to feel as strongly about acne as you feel about bankruptcy. It is a conceit that grows with age to 'look down' on younger people's problems. This is by way of saying, "You ain't seen nuthin' yet!" There is no known scale to measure the relative severity of problems. The only gauge is how a problem affects its possessor. So you are making a grave mistake to 'put down' a young person's problem.

That's *your* perspective. In their view, it's as bad as it can get. Telling them it's trivial just adds a layer of frustration to their burden. Sometimes that's enough to send them off the deep end.

Problems are strange things in another respect: one weighs no more than many. A single problem will worry you no more nor less than a half-dozen because, after all, you can only worry about one at a time. If there's only one, you will concentrate on it all the time. When you've got a whole list to worry about you simply divide your worrying time between them.

The reason you'll never be rid of problems is because of the way you and everyone else play the game of life. The rules state that *what isn't is more important (desirable) than what is.* You don't have to be a genius to figure out that what you are and what you have is much less when compared to what you are not and have not. Ergo, what we lack makes an endless shopping list, whereas what we have can be listed on the back of a calling card. Not only is the minus column endless, we tend to devalue our positive assets. "If I have it, it must not be worth much." Or, "If I can do it, it must not be anything special."

Familiarity breeds contempt

The trapeze artist is not amazed at his derring-do any more than a surgeon is thunderstruck at what his fingers can accomplish. We do tend to depreciate and take for granted what we do or have while being terribly impressed or covetous of our neighbor's possessions and abilities. Because no one individual can match the sum total of everyone else's accomplishments and acquisitions, most of us find ourselves lacking practically everything. This opens the door to dissatisfaction, the stuff of which too many problems are made.

Of course, desiring what isn't requires a knowledge of what we're missing. Said differently, discontent is caused by an awareness of alternatives. It's when you see displays of other people's wealth that your poverty becomes a 'problem.' Which explains why 'dissatisfaction' is so rampant in the electronic age. TV alone rubs hundreds of millions of faces in what they lack. Fifty years ago, a Georgia sharecropper had little or no contact with the world beyond his peanut patch. Now he knows all about the Lifestyles Of The Rich & Famous. His kids, likewise. This isn't all bad, of course. (For every 'bad,' there's a commensurate 'good.') Matter of fact, being aware of other possibilities can provide the impetus for improving the quality of one's life. You've got to know you're in jail, that there is an 'outside,' before you can value and obtain your freedom.

Time and place problems

Every age and generation has problems not shared by those who came before, or those who will follow. The problems associated with these times are quite different than those of your parent's time. Appreciating this relativity helps put our problems into some kind of mitigating perspective. A few hundred years ago, American males worried less about hair loss than the loss of their scalps. You think you had problems when you were young? How about today's youth?! Their futures are booby trapped with drugs, AIDS, a poisoned atmosphere, nuclear proliferation, polluted oceans, melting ice caps, stray bullets and AWOL parents.

Many problems are relative to 'place.' Freedom (of thought, expression and movement) is a problem in that place called China. Just as there are a bunch of problems unique to this place we call home. Such as homelessness.

No pain, no gain.

Some experts on the human condition would have you believe problems are an integral part of the human drama; necessary for growth. Just as lifting weights help muscles grow, handling problems helps your humanity grow.

This would suggest that carrying problems, like lifting weights, is a pain. Yes and no. It all depends on your carrying technique.

The slightest problem is enough to bring some people to their knees. While others skip through life seemingly unaware of their burdens. If they have a secret, you'll find it in the next chapter.

CHAPTER IX

LIGHTENING THE LOAD

Smiling in the Face of Adversity

Burdens become unbearable when you think you're going to be rid of them around every next corner. Once you accept the fact that if it isn't one thing it'll be another, you can develop a posture for carrying your allotted load through life without bending and breaking.

Weak backs and strong minds.

Age has something to do with our ability to handle problems. As our backs become weaker, we need to start using our heads.

By rights our mental muscles should be in tip-top shape after fiftysomething years of arduous exercise. Trouble is, too many of us have been flexing the wrong side of our minds—i.e., the left side which deals with Reality I.

People who have a way of smiling in the face of adversity operate in a different sphere. The signals they send and receive are on a higher frequency. These folks seem to know, consciously or intuitively, they are 'above' the problems encountered on the Reality I level. That is, their Reality II consciousness—their inner 'I Am'—is detached from the Reality I fray. From this position they're able to dispassionately observe the goings-on.

Elevating your consciousness

'Rising above' doesn't ignore, deny or minimize a problem. A person can be serene even in the face of great pain or certain death. Because he knows this isn't happening to the self that counts—the cosmic or immortal self. It's this level of consciousness that can rise above the mortal battlefield to observe the physical or ego-self at war.

This is done simply by realizing there are two you's. The action-oriented, material you who becomes embroiled in Reality I and pays the price with a bloody nose and bruised ego. And the witnessing you who observes what's happening to the embroiled you. So long as your higher consciousness is observing, you are not totally attached to the problem.

Again, this is not to deny what's happening on the physical, Reality I plane. But when you know it's possible to loose a leg without loosing any part of the essential, inner you—you can survive *anything*.

To be totally caught up in a problem is to loose control (of your self). You become a victim, a leaf in the wind, blown hither and thither by physical forces beyond your control. That's what anger and violence does.

Witnessing

Controlling a problem requires emotional detachment; viewing it dispassionately as an objective witness would.

To bear witness to a problem is to discuss it with your self or your God—it amounts to the same thing. That's all witnessing is. It works not so much because of what you said to your self, but because you stopped to 'discuss' it. That proves there's a part of you that stays detached from the action. You discuss what's happening as it happens.

All this is just so much theory, of course. It only counts if it can be and will be put into practice.

For example

Take a silly, inconsequential problem; the kind of thing that upsets people's serenity on a daily basis. You're late for a very important date with a hairdresser. (If your hair needs no 'dressing,' substitute Golf Pro or Accountant.) To make matters worse, you took a shortcut over a two-lane back road that put you behind a Motorhome wallowing along at 28 M.P.H. There's no place to pass. Your stomach is churning. Your head starts to throb. Why doesn't the S.O.B. pull over—can't he see me in his rearview? You are now beyond frustration. You begin to hate the driver. You hate all drivers of all Winnebagos. The situation leaves you with three choices. Try to pass and maybe kill yourself and/or others. Stay in line and get madder and madder as you become later and later. Or you can decide to experience what is happening to you; witness your self getting mad by describing how it's making your palms sweat and head ache. Ask your self, is it a pointed, sharp pain or a dull, blunt ache? Is it purplish or flaming red? Now feel the way the back of your neck is tensed; notice you've got the wheel in a death grip. And, Hey! In the process of observing your reactions, the anger and misery is out of mind.

You can't be angry while observing your anger. Also, when you concentrate on what's happening to you in the present (mad-ness), you can't focus on what's going to happen in the future (late-ness). You've detached your self from the problem. And in the process, your headache disappeared, your grip loosened, your neck relaxed and the Winnebago overheated and pulled over. (When you finally arrive, what d'ya bet your hairdresser/pro/accountant is even later than you?!)

Another everyday example, albeit potentially much more serious. Your doctor calls after reviewing your annual chest X-Rays. Instead of saying "Everything looks normal," he asks you to go come in tomorrow for more pictures. "Is there something wrong?" you ask. He says it's probably the X-Ray technician's mistake. "Nothing to be concerned about." But of course you're plenty concerned. What did he mean by "probably?" "What kind of mistake?" You've got 27 hours to work yourself into a lather. You begin to feel something in one lung; just a little something you don't think you've felt before. You breathe deep and it feels more so. It may be you're just imagining it. Maybe yes, maybe no.

You turn to what you were doing before the doctor called. Even while you're doing it, your mind wanders back to your chest. The rest of that day you go through the motions of living while thinking the worst. How will you react when the doc tells you the bad news? How will the family handle it? Will there be much pain? Think of the expense! What about your will? Where are the keys to the Safety Deposit box?

Get a grip on yourself

At this rate you'll be a basket case come tomorrow. You gotta get a grip on your self. But your mind keeps running out of control. Because you let it. Rather than tell your self what might happen, take note of what *is* happening; the inner self witnessing the outer self reacting. Observe the process. Notice the affect on your stomach. Feel your heart speed up. While you're doing that, you aren't thinking the thoughts that cause those effects.

Many times during this process you'll stop witnessing and begin worrying again. Take control again. It's like any battle. You gain some ground. Then fall back a bit. Gain more. In the end, you'll control the battlefield.

Notice this process didn't solve anything. If you had a problem before you detached your self from it; you'll still have it afterwards. But now that problem isn't feeding on itself; it isn't controlling your mind and dominating your mood. Just as chivalry keeps warfare within bounds, this process of detachment does the same for personal crises. Use it to keep a lid on panic or to salve life's minor irritations.

No fetal positions are required; no mantras or other mysterious regimes. It's just you, being you.

CHAPTER X

NOW IS FOREVER

Making Your Life an Endless Series of Beginnings

Time, as noted in Chapter 3, is a tricky business. In a metaphysical, Reality II context, the present is continuous, without end.

In our three-dimensional (Reality I) world, time is a man-made contrivance measuring that period occupied by a body passing in space from one given point to another.

Reconciling these two realities has occupied the most brilliant minds since time immemorial. The relativity of time is the crux of all quantum enquiries, from Einstein to Hawking.

The arrow of time

That sense we have of going from past to future is based on what physicists call "the thermodynamic arrow of time," what causes things to go from 'order' to 'disorder' (why ice melts and glass shatters). This thermodynamic arrow is the product of the cosmological arrow let loose by the Big Bang. The universe began infinitely hot, smooth and dense. Because there is no equilibrium in that perfect state, it had to change—i.e., move. The only direction it could head was from low entropy to tropy to greater entropy; from order to disorder: expanding, cooling, becoming lumpier and generally messier. This process created space and time as we have come to know it.

Backwards into the future.

In his best seller, 'A Brief History Of Time,' Stephen Hawking proposes the possibility there is no beginning and no end—i.e., no 'time.' A neat way to dodge the 'singularity' notion and beg basic conundrums, like 'What preceded the Big Bang?', 'Who/what created The Creator?', 'What's outside the Universe?' This addendum to The Big Bang theory suggests the universe expands and contracts ad infinitum (producing the inescapable conclusion that half the time, time is reversing itself—i.e., moves backward, from 'old' to 'young,' 'end' to 'beginning.') Else that volatile speck of primordial dust emanated from nothing, making the Creator a vacuum.

Before after

Reason supports the 'no beginning, no end' theory, notwithstanding the legions of theologians and physicists who insist otherwise. It patently is illogical, even nonsensical, to say a beginning can have no end. That which doesn't end can't begin. (For that reason Hindus believe the immortal soul is not created by God individually, one by one, but is birthless.) Likewise, to acknowledge the act of creation is to deny the Creator immortality. Or, not to put too fine a point on it,

it is denying the act of creation—and the Creator—
to say the Universe (all reality, subjective and objective) is destined to end. You can't make nothing out of
something. The architect would disappear with the
architecture.

It is equally illogical to believe the universe will continue to expand forever outward. Or, somehow settle into
a static state of equilibrium; an equally improbable scenario. Energy, whether sound or light, is transmitted in
waves characterized by high and low points. Therein lies
the rhythm of the Universe; the essential Yin and Yang:
up/down; in/out; hot/cold ad infinitum.

There can be no Yin without Yang; no beauty without ugliness; no 'up' without a corresponding 'down.' 'Out'
cannot exist without an 'in.' Verily, a 'beginning' requires
an 'end' (unless it is an endless series of beginnings).

The universe in all its aspects is cyclic and circular. A
straight line must eventually meet itself coming back!
Everything that goes around comes around!

The conclusion is inescapable. The only way to avoid
an end, is to deny a beginning ... which gets us back to
the eternal NOW.

All this may be interesting, but a bit removed from
The Art Of Linear Living. Or is it?

Living in the present

Timelessness, as a metaphysical concept, tells us the
past and the future are illusions. Reality only occurs in
The Present. And that NOW goes on endlessly.

"A person is afraid of growing old to the extent that he is not really living now."
—C.G. Jung

Yet in our objective, three-dimensional (Reality I) world, the form we call our body is not immortal.

NOW remains constant, but observable objects obey physical laws and change their properties over time. (Dust to dust.) Our material form is allotted a limited number of quantitative NOWs. To make the most of them, we must not allow disturbing memories or future fears to pollute the potentially perfect present. There's an art to actualizing the 'pregnant moment,' more of a technique, really. One needs to fill the moments of his/her life with significant, meaningful (as in memorable) events. To do this, one must be master of his/her time versus mastered by time—what happens when you 'spend' or 'pass' time, blotting it out with sleep, drugs, TV or a variety of other desensitizing pastimes.

Right NOW is perfect

You aren't in any kind of pain right NOW, are you? You aren't starving to death, or having a lung removed at this very moment.

You may have just received word that an inappropriate tax deduction requires you to visit the IRS at some later date—but the fact remains, right NOW, as you read this page, everything's okay (or you wouldn't be reading).

Maybe yesterday wasn't okay, maybe you won't be okay an hour from now, much less on Tuesday next when your IRS visit is scheduled. But right NOW, there's nothing wrong, right?

You can be unemployed with no means to make the next mortgage payment. If that makes you feel non-okay, it's because you're anticipating a moment when you won't be feeling okay. But that's not NOW. That will be when the phone rings and someone from the Savings & Loan threatens foreclosure. And even when that horrible moment arrives and it turns out to be exactly the way you feared it would be—that NOW will be so filled with activity, you won't be asking yourself if it's good or bad. You'll be busy handling the situation.

People don't stop in the middle of a battle, after receiving a gunshot wound in the shoulder, and say, "Hey! This NOW is no good." Those few NOWs that are not okay take care of themselves—they are action NOWs. The NOWs we dote on are the private, passive and contemplative NOWs, all of which are perfectly good NOWs… if they remain unpolluted. And yet those controllable NOWs are the ones that get out of control to make us miserable.

The lesson here is don't use the present to fear the future or regret the past.

This does not mean we do not have to deal with the past or provide for the future in the present. What would happen to Mr. Squirrel come winter if he didn't scurry around collecting nuts in the Fall? For sure he wouldn't last until Spring. Making provisions for the future doesn't mess up the present.

"Don't look back, something might be gaining on you."
—Satchel Paige

"If we shouldn't look back and can't look forward, the conclusion is obvious: seize the day."
—Eli Rubinstein

81

Squirrels seem to enjoy the process for its own sake. Buying life insurance should be a pleasure, not a pain. An archeologist finds pleasure and satisfaction digging into the past.

Beginning NOW

As a moment in time, NOW is a clean slate, completely neutral, always open to any possibility. This is true at '2' or '92.' Every NOW is a beginning, a springboard, the point from which all possibilities proceed—the penultimate opportunity.

The old saw, "Today is the first day of the rest of your life" is right-on. You are always at a point when any future can overtake you.

Yet the older we are, the more we measure our value based on the time we have left. Never, ever succumb to that good-for-nothing feeling. As long as you can lift a thought, much less a finger, you must act on every NOW. Do not be misled by a culture which presumes nothing new and exciting ever happens to 'old' folks. To the degree that is true, is the degree 'old' people fulfill those expectations by inaction; resisting anything new and exciting.

The next chapters will try to save you from that fate.

NOTES TO MYSELF

CHAPTER XI

SONG OF THE OPEN ROAD

Press On, Regardless

At fiftysomething, you've reached the crest of that proverbial hill. Your past life stretches out behind you, and ahead a sign reading 'Retirement' marks life's next main intersection.

Once at the top, the rest of the way looks easy. This leads a lot of people to put their lives in Neutral and try coasting the rest of the way ... only to loose their momentum a few years down the road. Others put the pedal to the metal and disappear in a cloud of dust ... only to lose control upon overtaking the slowpokes.

Not to worry. Some baling wire and Bandaids have you on the road again.

Critical crossroads

As you reach '65' a crossroads sign flashes up ahead.

No one approaches this juncture without some trepidation. This is no place to make a wrong turn because all the roads past this point are one-way. There are signs aplenty pointing the way to various objectives: 'This Way To Adventure,' 'Straight Ahead To Serenity,' 'For Salvation Bear Right,' but no indication what travails may be encountered en route, no guarantees the destinations will be as marked.

And wouldn't you agree, a great number of travellers would, given the opportunity, beg the question of 'whither to?' and pull over at the first sign of a comfort station a.k.a. retirement community.

Circle the wagons

They are a curious phenomenon, these in-gatherings of senior citizens. What started as caravans of Winnebagos forming protective circles at road's end, have become walled cities, insulated from the clash of cultures colliding beyond their gates.

It is easy enough to understand the allure of these retreats. Anyone a bit weary from that long climb up the hill, especially those loaded with loot collected along the way, is easily detoured with promises of perpetual R&R, particularly when all roads ahead disappear into a haze hiding who-knows-what kind of unpleasantness. Only the hardiest time traveller can resist pulling out of the fast lane and disappearing behind those locked gates forevermore.

Echoes

Those who succumb will find themselves surrounded by nothing but themselves. All their aches and complaints will be endlessly repeated on the first tee and at High Tea. Protecting their persons and property will be the principal card table conversation, while their worst fears and anxieties are reinforced and fulfilled at free seminars platforming conservative journalists lecturing on the evils of homophobic miscegenation. The lack of diversity keeps argument to a minimum and breeds a benign indifference to tolerance. Nothing unexpected or unsterilized is allowed to invade these precincts and those who leave usually head for a cruise ship where their fellow passengers are carbon copies of the friends they left behind.

How fossils are formed

People who stop their forward progress at sixty or sixty-five develop the Inertia Syndrome. Lack of movement coincides with an absence of controversy which increases the aversion to contrary opinions. This in turn lowers the resistance to fault-finding until the patient is totally rigid.

The first sign is a contraction of neck and shoulder muscles causing the sufferer to hunch, cave inward as it were, in the manner of one who wishes to present a more difficult target for the slings and arrows hurled from the other side of the wall. In its final stages, the Inertia Syndrome will fossilize its victims; make them totally impervious to outside influences. In this condition, any attempt to dent their consciousness only glances off their granite-like exteriors leaving not the slightest impression.

There is nothing inherently wrong about assuming such a defensive posture. However, the effects it causes are not anyone's idea of a good time. Remember, the mind programs the body—i.e., thoughts create corresponding external conditions.

Thoughts are things

People who spend most of their waking hours in a preventative, fearful mode, to protect their persons and property against real or imagined trespassers, will have little time or capacity for pleasure. Their demeanor is typically stern and suspicious, calculated to keeps strangers at arm's length and warn friends and neighbors not to take advantage. A barrel of fun they are not! It affects not just their attitude but their appearance, *and health!* As a man (or woman) thinketh ... to wit:

- **The subjective mind is the builder, and the destroyer, of the body.**
- **Our body represents the aggregate of our beliefs.**
- **Nature obeys us precisely in proportion as we first obey Nature.**
- **Every thought is as powerful as a deed, and in many cases far more effective than any word or weapon.**
- **You cannot think without a result.**

Exodus

As described, the Inertia Syndrome only attacks people in their latter years, and those attacks most frequently strike the inhabitants of senior enclaves. This has caused many retirees to abandon their walled citadels and once again take their chances on the open road.

Apologia

To be sure, not all retirement community residents suffer these effects. The exceptions are not the rule, however. It is not easy to march to your inner drummer in somebody else's parade.

In all fairness it also must be said that the proliferation of retirement communities and their ancillaries, continuing care facilities, is not so much caused by a lack of heart among the inhabitants as due to changes in the woof and wrap of this country's social fabric.

The contemporary family is not a cohesive unit. Our villages are global, our relatives far-flung, and our homes seldom are large enough to accommodate elders. So elders must accommodate themselves. Their first move is into something more manageable in size and design, with electronic eyes in place of sons and daughters.

Those who would eschew the institutionalized version of retirement living in favor of something more individualized risk isolation and idleness, two problems that are solved in the next chapter.

CHAPTER XII

DAMN THE TORPEDOES

This Is No Time To Play It Safe

After fiftysomething people tend to hold their cards close to the vest. "I'm too old to take chances," is the usual rationale. A reasonable reaction to aging, or is it?

What's the difference between the malnourished miser whose cookie jar is stuffed with Treasury Bills and those seniors who park their lives in a predictable continuum.

You can't conserve time.

You can't *save* time, hoarding it like some commodity.

Saving is the antithesis of using. The ultimate conservation is utilization.

Young people, those with the most (years) to loose, act like there's no tomorrow. While the people with the least to loose, are disposed to waste it doing nothing. Or suspend it with reverie or sleep.

That's only natural, up to a point. The point at which it becomes unnatural is when teenagers go over the edge and old people won't go near it.

Acting conservatively, to avoid waste, is a good thing. It becomes a bad thing when 'conservative' becomes 'de-

- - ◂█▸ - -

GRANNIES PUT PEDALS TO THEIR METTLES

Boda, Norway—Uuni Brinch-
man spent all her life fearing
heights. At 58 she bailed out
of a small plane at 12,000 feet.
Voluntarily.

Brinchman was one of a group
of grannies to endure a two-
hour open boat ride to Old
Woman Island 50-miles above
the Arctic Circle where they
danced under the midnight sun
celebrating a three-day Grandmother Festival. Besides jumping out of airplanes, they raced
cars, horses and boats. Why?
According to their spokes-
woman, Ann Kerr, a 61-year
old grandmother of three who
sailed her sloop across the At-
lantic to attend the festival, "We
are at a stage when we can
take risks."

- - ◂█▸ - -

fensive.' When you fear the loss of something (whether it's financial security or your life), you have effectively lost it!

Meaningful moments

Some moments are more significant than others. Motoring across a featureless plain is a boring way to spend time. (Note the use of 'spend,' which suggests the activity was costly, or unprofitable.) The driver is inclined to activate 'Cruise Control' and spend the time 'somewhere else,' thinking about where he's been or where he's going, for-example. While the passenger dozes (until some significant scenery come into view). When they arrive at their destination, little will be remembered about those featureless hours ... the same way we remember little of those hours we spend performing daily routines, like commuting. But if another car suddenly crashes in front of yours, requiring a dramatic maneuver to avoid disaster—that moment is forever etched on your memory.

Edgework

The more humdrum or programmed our existence, the more we are driven to introduce some risk into our lives—explaining the popularity of rock-climbing and bungee jumping. There are more positive and constructive ways to make more of your moments meaningful and memorable, however.

We aren't talking about 'cheap thrills' here. *Intensity* is the objective. As e.e. cummins said, "A man who lives intensely really lives."

The more you are able to direct your life consciously, the more you'll remain focused on the present.

Contrariwise, the more conformist, undifferentiated and unfree you are, the more you will be a slave to quantitative time, living by the clock, driven by compulsion rather than choice, acting like a robot rather than a creature possessing free will. The most unfree kind of existence undoubtedly is led by prisoners. They 'serve time' who spend it in jail. Yet how many of us spend our time as if in jail? How many hours have you 'killed' in meaningless (and thoughtless) endeavors? How many years have you spent vicariously, in front of a TV?

Security vs. intensity

If there is one thing lacking in the lives of older/aged people, it's that essential quality, *intensity.*

The idealized senior lifestyle eliminates risk and chance, without which there is very little intensity. As you approach your sixties, you are expected to 'act your age.' This means trade in the motorcycle, stop rolling the dice and work towards a future devoid of uncertainty and hardship.

When it comes time to occupy that velvet-lined rut, you'll find it a living death. Strong words, but at the very least, too much security dulls your edge and leaves you feeling flat and bored; a candidate for debilitating depression.

Quantity vs. Quality

People who become preoccupied with avoiding risks, whether physical or financial, are likely to isolate themselves in the safety of an antiseptic cocoon designed to keep out anything that threatens the status quo. Walls, gates, guards, Dobermans, air filters, bottled waters present a sorry spectacle if they result in an empty life devoid of challenge and satisfaction.

Take a look at the tack your life is taking. If you're headed for a snug harbor where you can ride out old age with nary a wave to disturb your tranquility, now is the time to change course. Sailboats are for sailing and life is for living. Better to go down at sea than gather barnacles at anchor.

Money matters

None of this means throwing caution to the wind. Wealth, like health, matters. What you do with it matters as well. People who spend their time defending their assets are not using them. Wealth can set you free or put you in solitary confinement for the rest of your days.

Many of us reach retirement age with empty bank accounts. People in this position are not likely to con-

sider themselves fortunate. Never-
theless, they never become a prisoner to their possessions. They
remain in the competitive world,
challenged by uncertainty to the end
of their days ... which are likely to
last longer as a result! Being a pro-

"Amass a store of gold and
jade, and no one can pro-
tect it."

—Lao-tsu

"The less you got, the less
you got to loose."

—Dylan

ductive member of society into your seventies and eight-
ies gives you what your better-heeled peers lack: intensity and focus. You will spend your time in the present
and be better off for it. And unless you succumb to resentments and regrets, and envy your peers' leisure, you
will find a way to provide for your needs notwithstanding the real and imagined handicaps of age. (As covered
in chapter 2, your experience and work ethic will become increasingly in demand as our technocratic society approaches the 21st century.)

It's never too late

The longevity revolution makes 'starting over' possible, not only for the fiftysomething contingent, but for
many years thereafter. In all likelihood you've already
made a couple or three career changes. (The current crop
of college grads will have five careers in their lifetimes, it
is predicted.) So it's never too late to switch fields or
pursue some lifelong ambition. There are plenty of examples to inspire you. Julia Child started her culinary
career in her late fifties. Congresswoman Millicent
Fenwick won her first election at 65. You already know

what Grandma Moses accomplished in her latter years. Going further back, Michaelangelo started the Medici Chapel at fifty-five.

Once more into the breech, Horatio

The reason these late starters stand out as 'exceptions' is that too few elderly people attempt to restart their lives. We're inclined to follow the well-worn script that if we haven't 'made it' by fifty or sixty, forget it. After that, few succeed because few try. Anything can happen in ten or twenty years. Or nothing can happen. It is entirely up to you.

The itch for change and challenge is part of the human condition, and for most of us it seems to increase with age. If you haven't scratched it before now, don't deny your self that pleasure much longer.

Those who don't want to or have to generate income in their later years can concentrate on finding a contributory role, or seeking fulfillment through personal accomplishment.

It doesn't have to be something dramatic or physically risky like jumping off a cliff strapped to a hang glider or single-handedly circumnavigating the globe. One retiree was determined to walk every street in his city. Another couple joined a commune. Some go back to school full-time to satisfy an interest or develop a talent. There's teaching. And preaching. Mentorship. Piano lessons, The Peace Corps, politics and Good Causes of all sorts (including the Communitarian movement). Whatever it is, it should require total commitment, taking your mind off your self so you don't spend the rest of your life fretting about the shape of your liver, a son's divorce or the Federal Deficit.

Fate/Karma deals us certain cards with which to play the game of life. Holding yours close to the vest, unwilling to lay down even one, is not playing the game. Those who stand pat become bored to death, literally.

DO SOMETHING, FOR A CHANGE

Looking for a cause, some meaningful way to give back some of the quality of life you've enjoyed to date? There is nothing more basic and critical than nursing our sick planet back to health. When you contribute to that, you're helping every living soul, including those who won't be born if the status quo is not drastically altered in the next forty years (which neatly coincides with your present life expectancy).

Risking failure

No one likes loosing. But they're only chips, after all. If you don't use them now, there's no taking them with you.

Anyway, a loosing hand is not a lost cause. Without losers there would be no winners. Both outcomes require players!

So what are you waiting for? Pump up those Nikes and *just do it.*

CHAPTER XIII

PUTTING WISDOM TO WORK IN THE TRENCHES

Now That You've Got Some You're Obliged To Share It

I f there is a reward for longevity, it is paid out in the form of wisdom, a quality of consciousness that has little to do with intelligence/I.Q. or book learning. "It is the characteristic of wisdom," said Thoreau, "not to do desperate things." Paul Baltes, Co-Director of the Max Planck Institute for Human Development in Berlin, puts it even more succinctly, "Wisdom has no extremes." It is the stuff of Aristotle's Golden Mean.

Being a by-product of experience, wisdom more often is possessed by men and women who have survived fifty or more winters. Indeed, the aforementioned Institute claims wisdom can be measured much in the same way intelligence is gauged. And those measurements have confirmed that more wisdom resides on the plus side of fifty than the minus side, with the highest marks recorded around sixty.

You can't eat wisdom

Wisdom, however, doesn't (necessarily) put food on the table. What's rewarding about the benignity of wisdom is it makes us nicer mammals, fostering a mellow outlook, a tolerance of uncertainty, and the inclination to pay attention to others—characteristics that contribute to a happier, healthier old age. The latter benefit—paying attention to others—is worthy of closer scrutiny.

Wisdom only can be actualized through the sharing of it. Other human qualities, such as talent, can be enjoyed in isolation. (True, musicians or painters, and even writers, receive more pleasure as well as manna when they share their talent with an audience. Yet artists receive pleasure when hearing/seeing themselves do good work.)

Wisdom retained is wisdom wasted

Wisdom is expressed by means of the written or spoken word (preferably the latter). The function of language is for the exchange or sharing of information. Thus wisdom requires a giver and one or more receivers. And it is up to the receiver(s) to decide if what the giver has given qualifies as wise. A would-be 'Wise Man' who sits contemplating his navel on some wind-swept Himalayan crag cannot be considered wise until he is joined by one or more others who will certify his words as wise. Unless or until that exchange happens the guru is no different from the unheard sound of a falling tree. Has it indeed made a sound? Fallen?

Who needs it?

It would follow that those of us who have acquired a modicum of wisdom are obliged to share it. The question is: with whom? If those most in need are those most lacking in wisdom, the younger generation in general and teenagers in particular would seem the preferred recipients. But as any wise man or woman well knows, teenagers have an aversion, something approaching a psychological allergy to any information (especially in the form of advice) coming from anyone over thirty. Whether or not this is evidence of Nature's contrariness or a cultural aberration — there are ways to lower teenagers' resistance. These ways have to do with packaging: the manner and means of sharing.

In primitive societies, elders held regularly scheduled counsels with the tribe's pubescent members.

Collective wisdom was inculcated by means of formal ritual and informal strolls in the forest.

The closest our modern society comes to fostering similar associations are mentorship programs sponsored by do-gooding organization like churches, service clubs, civic groups and ethnic assemblies of one sort or another. These are good as far as they go. Trouble is, they don't go far enough. The extant mentorship programs seldom reach the young people most in need and most at-risk: inner city youth. Their need to belong and be counted is filled by rum-amok gangs whose savage ethos have turned our urban centers into howling jungles. Misguided Welfare programs encourage poverty-level fathers to go AWOL creating a values vacuum of such proportions that even the most ambitious mentorship program would seem to be an exercise in futility. But a journey of a thousand miles must begin with the first step. That step might just be a supplement to the standard juvenile probation produres now is place at various detention centers; an out-reach effort initiated by a caring cadre of community elders. The program might work like this: When a young offender is released from custody on probation, he or she is assigned a volunteer mentor with whom the probationer is required, on penalty of being sent back to the Detention Center, to spend a minimum amount of time with—say a half a day a week. This time would not be used in preaching, teaching or any other kind of advice-giving. The elder's function, in the beginning, would be less an advisor and more a non-judgmental listener (a role requiring a great deal of wisdom!) who lends an empathetic ear to whatever is on the young person's mind.

In most cases these troubled teens are not going to be too forthcoming; probably they'll resent like hell these mandatory sessions. It may take many weeks, maybe months, before there is any kind of relationship with enough trust to encourage the teenager to solicit the elder's opinion. The terms of the association would control the kind and extent of any help the mentor might wish to volunteer. These are details, however important.

Once the probationary requirements have been met, it's up to the two parties as to the future, if any, of the relationship. The fact it is a volunteer effort, devoid of selfish interest, sends a message that many young people never before have received. Someone really does care. Someone not driven by fear, duty, anger or ambition wants to help. A disestablished someone devoid of the trappings of authority. Sort of a surrogate grandparent.

It goes without saying that 99% of the time, a black man will better relate to a black boy than a white woman.

Early intervention

This concept might also be applied as a preventative measure, working with advocacy organizations, inner city agencies (including the police department) and youth groups, even organized gangs. Or, in the case of first-time offenders, it could be applied as a substitute for incarceration.

The flipside of puberty

Such a program's foundation rests on the mentor's 'senior' status. People past sixty are no threat to someone sixteen—for the same reason grand children and grandparents get-along: they have a common enemy!

Certainly elder wisdom can be put to no better use than to help those who will be at the controls of Spaceship Earth as it enters a new millennium. No other effort is apt to produce such meaningful results. Teenagers, no matter however troubled they may be, are a lot closer to making their lives work than most adults; closer by virtue of not having had time to go far wrong.

The mold is hardening, but not yet set.

You can't lose

And whether or not you see any positive results produced from your mentorship, you will receive two payoffs: 1) associating with young people keeps you young in heart, and 2) When your mind is filled with someone else's problems there's no room to grow your own.

That second payoff is by far the most valuable. For this is the time of life when your vocation or profession occupies less of your mind—leaving more and more room to entertain the anxieties that go with aging. (These concerns tend to expand in direct proportion to the amount of attention paid to them.) At this time of life, serving others serves your best interests. And what better way to counter seniors' selfish image than to be a benefactor instead of beneficiary; a patron rather than patronized.

"If to be old is not to be wise, then it is simply to be obsolete."
—Page Smith

In a culture that does not seek the counsel of its elder members, such a program would provide the missing rostrum. Becoming advocates for this country's most valuable (and endangered) resource is as worthwhile a cause as any you could undertake.

Gatekeepers

Countering the disposition of young and old to live in different worlds and maintaining continuity between generations is the traditional role of society's senior citizens. "Social intercourse between generations," observed John Jay Chapman, "is the basis for any civilized society."

In a variation on this theme, Marty Knowlton, the founder of Elderhostel (a worldwide educational program for seniors), has established a non-profit organization called Gatekeepers to the Future, dedicated to "the preservation and restoration of the earth and all its life."

No one is better equipped to be custodians of the Good Earth than those most familiar with it (and those most responsible for its present condition). By harnessing seniors' resources, knowledge, skills *and wisdom*, Knowlton has created a corps of solicitors for the otherwise unrepresented future generations.

Opening the tap

The amount of wisdom presently going to waste in those wretched retirement compounds is an indictment of both the retirees and those who would benefit from their counsel. Dr. Ken Dychtwald, a Berkeley gerontologist and psychologist (who has worked for the California Department of Aging) acknowledges, "We've done a poor job creating opportunities for contribution by older people. Instead of asking what can we (the non-old public) do for the elderly, we should concentrate on providing the elderly with opportunities to do things for us, and for themselves."

It's a win/win situation when a society involves its seniors in the activities and interests of its junior members. The juniors gain invaluable counsel and services for little or nothing. The seniors gain self-esteem and a marked reduction in physical and emotional aches and complaints. Usefulness is a powerful preventative medicine.

NOTES TO MYSELF

CHAPTER XIV

TO YOUR GOOD HEALTH

As a Man Thinketh (Part 2)

What follows by no means is an all-encompassing overview on the subject of health, much less health in later life. Rather it is an arbitrary selection of esoteric and unconventional wisdom on the subject that is out of print, out of style or otherwise out of reach to the uninitiated.

Read and reap:

Meditate, don't vegetate

A mellow outlook—being more calm, tolerant—helps the body last longer. A study compared seniors (average age 81) who practiced transcendental meditation with a randomly selected non-practicing control group. Everyone in the TM group was alive after three years, while 37.5% of the do-nothing group had died.

The researchers didn't have to look far to find the reasons for this. TM produces a sharp increase in the alpha rhythm, a decrease in the breathing rate and oxygen consumption, pulse and blood pressure, with an increase in the electrical resistance of the skin. There is also a dramatic drop in the level of lactate in the blood

—high levels being associated with stress—that persists long after meditation ceases.

Another study, reported in a highly respected medical journal, went so far as to conclude people who meditate live 5 to 10 years longer.

The mental state producing these remarkable results may be described as 'restful alertness.' While usually associated with religious or spiritual contemplation, any technique of conscious control of involuntary functions, including biofeedback, that induces this state of mind will produce the same result.

Laugh your cares away

The anatomy of melancholy is well documented. Chronic stress and its compatriots, hostility, anger and depression can sicken and even kill us by producing surges of adrenaline, noradrenaline and cortisol that sear the body like dribbling acid.

You can reduce or eliminate stress, the cause of that destructive dribble, by inducing laughter and harder-to-monitor sensations like optimism, curiosity and rapture. These not only make life worth living, but also make it last longer.

There are a bundle of studies that attest to the results produced. But science knows little about *why* happiness is healthy. What little is known revolves around two compounds. The best-known one, endorphins, is the brain's indigenous opium. This is one and the same chemical that gives joy to long-distance runners. The other is oxytocin, a hormone secreted by the pituitary gland that seems to mediate feelings of satisfaction and harmony.

Little more is know about these behavioral resources because the medical industry's focus is fixed on what makes people sick versus what makes them happy. By this logic, happiness is an antidote for anxiety rather than a preventative. Also, happiness is not a state of mind that lends itself to scientific research. With one exception, it's difficult to induce experimental states of happiness in a laboratory environment. That exception is laughter.

Sustained hilarity, among other things, is an agreeable form of aerobic exercise. When laughter subsides, blood pressure and pulse fall to lower, more salubrious levels than before the fun began. According to a Stanford University researcher, one-hundred laughs is equal to 10 minutes of rigorous rowing.

Other tests indicate laughter can alleviate discomfort. A group of students watching a Bill Cosby show were able to endure a much more painful level of electrical shocks than a control group viewing a video about the care and feeding of hanging plants.

For more information about the healing power of laughter, consult Norman Cousins who laughed away his cancer and lived to write a book on the subject.

Acupuncture, anyone?
It wasn't long ago that this method of alleviating pain and correcting all manner of dysfunctional disorders was

right out of woo-woo land, on a level with crystal therapy and alchemy.

That was before Scotty Reston, then the NEW YORK TIMES' Washington correspondent, accompanied Nixon and Kissinger on their door-opening trip to Red China. While there, Reston fell ill, underwent abdominal surgery with acupuncture the only anesthesia.

Because he lived to tell about it, Westerners came to believe in it, to the point that today acupuncture is a common treatment regime throughout the U.S., albeit, few patients and/or their surgeons are willing to rely on it anywhere near to the extent they do in Asia where it is the anesthesia of choice for the most rigorous surgical procedures. In China, incidentally, the emphasis is on prevention of disease rather than treatment of the symptoms. (In the old days, a patient paid a doctor to keep him from becoming ill; if he did fall sick, the doctor paid him: try that on your HMO.)

The essence of acupuncture is the belief that all matter consists of two entities or activities, Yin and Yang, and that well-being depends on their proper balance. These two activities are manifest as subtle energy flows (called 'Chi' by the Chinese) circulating in the body which at some points come close enough to the surface to be manipulated. Those control points have been pinpointed and related to physiological functions over thousands of years of practice. Fingertip pressure or the insertion of a metal needle releases an excess of the appropriate energy.

Science is unable to explain the whys and wherefores of acupuncture. We know it works, and that's the main thing—at least for the patient. There is nothing in the way of a belief system involved, however, beyond that of support or reinforcement.

Using your head

Loss of mental acuity has less to do with the loss of neurons (as part of the intrinsic aging process) than with mental inactivity. It turns out those neurons can sprout new connections when stimulated. So the more you challenge/stimulate your brain, the more you increase the production of those new connections. While the brain is not a muscle, you might consider it so, the way it benefits from exercise. In other words, use it or lose it.

All this has created a new mini-industry called 'brain gyms,' where you're hooked up to a sound and light machine in the form of some spacey-looking stereo headphones and goggles attached to a small electronic controller. The headphones transmit sound patterns that pulse in rhythm with flickering red lights in the eyeglasses.

Users of these brain exercise machines claim, apparently with good reason, they reduce stress, engender a blissful, meditative state similar to the sensory deprivation experience produced in flotation tanks. More to the point, these new wave brain machines improve memory and accelerate learning. Researchers have found the machines can produce 20 point IQ improvements. The intelligence-boosting effect is produced by increasing the production of those critical neurochemicals.

If you're already too smart for your own good, one of these cerebral energizers probably are worth the price ($200 and up, or $7 an hour at a 'gym') for their stress-reducing properties. A mellow state of mind plays an important role in keeping the mind young. Tension releases hormones, called glucocorticoids, that act as a damper on that part of the brain dealing with memory and learning. Too many of those hormones, like too many screaming grandchildren, can make the brain old before its time. You can combat stress at the dinner table, too. Go on a low-fat, high-fiber diet with lots of exercise.

If you like to keep things simple, you can forego all this space-age stuff in favor of taking up a new hobby or different line of work. According to a Ph.D. named Ben Douglas, any kind of new activity stimulates brain neurons in different parts of the brain.

> "A mind always employed is always happy ... the idle are the only wretched."
> —Thomas Jefferson

Hands that heal

Most so-called 'Faith Healers,' like most mediums, clairvoyants, palm readers and other supernatural entrepreneurs, rely more on their client's gullibility than on extrasensory powers. But it only takes one exception to establish a case for a future rule.

To be a bona fide exception, a 'healer' would have to change his or her venue from a backwater tent to a laboratory presided over by credentialed scientists. For a report of one such case we quote from Dr. Lyall Watson's 1974 book, *Supernature.*

"Bernard Grad of McGill University has done pioneer work in this field. His subject was a faith healer who claimed to be able to cure disease by the biblical method of 'laying on of hands.' In a preliminary test involving three hundred mice with identical injuries, those held by the healer for fifteen minutes a day did in fact heal more quickly than those held by other people.

"Grad tried to expose this ability to more critical analysis by narrowing its effect in an ingenious experiment using barley seeds. The seeds were treated with salt and baked in an oven long enough to injure but not kill them. Then twenty seeds were planted in each of twenty-four flower pots and watered each day. The water used was taken directly from a tap into two sealed glass bottles, and each day the healer held one of these in his hands for thirty minutes. An experimental procedure was designed so that no person knew which plants were given the 'treated' water, but after two weeks it was found that those given the benefit of the healer's hand on their water supply were not only more numerous but also taller and gave a higher yield.

"Grad tested the water and found there was a slight spreading between the hydrogen and oxygen atoms. The change in what we know to be an unstable molecule was apparently triggered by the action of an individual human (electromagnetic) field. Following this clue, Grad tried to assess the personality involved in this healing response. He had water for a second barley-seed test treated by three different people. One was a psychiatrically normal man, one was a woman with a strong depressive neurosis, and the third was a man with psychotic delusional depression. The water treated by the normal man produced seeds that showed no difference from control ones, but the growth of seedlings that received water handled by the depressed patients was greatly retarded. The discovery of a negative as well as a positive response is important. It is conceivable, even in an experiment as carefully contrived as this one, that some factor could have been overlooked and that the positive result had nothing to do with the healer. But when a negative subject—a sick person—produces an appropriately negative response, then the original premise is greatly strengthened and the case for the healer looks good."

Green force fields

Watson goes on to offer evidence that the forces created by human energy fields also produce the 'green thumb' effect. This seemingly "magical ability to make things grow, while others using exactly the same methods and spending just as much time in their gardens end up with nothing but withered leaves and aphids. The good gardeners may generate a (energy) field that has a beneficial effect on plant growth. And it is by no means impossible that a variant of this (force) field could be equally beneficial to human beings." He says, "There are people who even in a crowd seem to radiate powerful goodwill or equally powerful evil. We are not a great deal nearer understanding this effect, but the experiments of Grad make it impossible to deny that such effects could exist. There seems to be almost no limit to the things that we can make our body do if we put our mind to it."

Warts wiped out

Dr. Watson offers skin diseases as further evidence that thought can effect matter by suggestion, in this case through the medium of common clinical hypnosis. "Warts seem to be most closely associated with psychological factors... In one well-controlled study, fourteen patients with long-standing warts all over their bodies were given suggestions that those on only one side of the body would disappear. In five weeks they did."

Antidote for allergies

Watson goes on to write that human "allergies seem to be similarly responsive to suggestion. An elegant test in Japan involved blindfolded subjects, all of whom were known to be allergic to chestnut trees. When the leaves were placed on their left arms and they were told that these were from the allergy producing tree, all developed the usual dermatitis; but when the same leaves were placed on their right arms and said to be harmless, no reaction took place. All allergic reaction is produced by a foreign substance, such as pollen, that enters the body and combines with a protein to form a specific antibody that sometimes produces distressing side effects or allergic reactions. It is a straightforward biochemical reaction that apparently has nothing to do with the brain, but there is now a wealth of evidence to show beyond doubt that this whole process is governed by mental factors.

There's more. "The classic test for TB, a bacterial infection, is the Mantoux test, which produces a red allergic weal on the skin if the patient has TB antibodies in his blood, but it has been shown that a hypnotic suggestion not to react can produce a negative response to the test even in someone riddled with tuberculosis. This nicely demonstrates the dominance of emotion over the wasting disease, which has long associations with depression and unrequited lovers 'alone and palely loitering.'"

Whether the results in these last examples were produced by hypnosis or by what others prefer to see as simple 'suggestion,' the fact remains, says the author, "all these bodily functions, which are normally operated by the autonomic nervous system, over which we have no conscious control, are amenable to outside influence. Whatever that process may be, it has enormous biological significance and gives us our first direct contact with the elusive unconscious."

Graphology
Handwriting analysis, in some people's minds, comes awfully close to palm reading—something you encounter in County Fairs and roadside shacks.

And yet many (more and more) employers now have handwriting analysts on their Human Resources staffs scrutinizing written applications for top management positions. While the efficacy of their gleanings may be controversial, there is no gainsaying the connection between health and handwriting. More than twenty-five years ago, the American Medical Association reported, "There are definite organic diseases that graphodiagnostics can help to diagnose from their earliest beginnings." The list includes anemia, blood poisoning, tumors, and various bone diseases. The AMA report contained the caveat that old age can produce substantially the same signs. Some skilled geriatricians use handwriting as a sort of X-ray to distinguish between actual mental unbalance and normal senility.

The healing mind

The mind or consciousness, not to be confused with brain (about which more follows), can and occasionally does accomplish everything that medical science and pharmacology is capable of, and ever so much more. The power of thought can move objects as well as to change their properties. Regrettably, mind power too often works to our disadvantage, producing negative results.

Because we're only beginning to understand how to control our consciousness in order to produce a certain outcome, mind power has remained an esoteric subject relegated to the realm of faith and hocus pocus. When the principles and processes are understood, they will be revealed not as exceptions to existing laws but as further evidence of the universal order at work.

Many U.S. doctors have crossed over to so-called 'Alternative' or holistic medicine, and the consensus is *every thought has a biochemical effect* (on the body). Medical research is teaming up with psychology to learn how the brain/mind converses with the body. ('Science' insists on understanding how a procedure works before recognizing it, whereas repeated results are enough to satisfy the Chinese.) The old medical paradigm treated the brain/mind as an independent processor. Now it's considered an interdependent part of the whole.

It is interesting to note neither the Chinese, Russians or the AMA has any working definition for the mind or consciousness as an entity separate from the brain. There is a general awareness that consciousness has 'a mind of its own.' Consciousness might be referred to as the brain's operating software—i.e., our brains do not so much produce consciousness as moderate and process it in the manner of a field effect. And until science can get a handle on where the brain stops and consciousness begins, defining soul and spirit will remain the province of metaphysics.

The greatest physician of them all
Meanwhile, as others reason why the rest of us would do well to take instruction from that pre-eminent and pioneering 'Mental Scientist,' Jesus Christ, who said (according to Mark xi. 24, R.V.), "*All things whatsoever ye pray*

and ask for, believe that ye **have** *received them, and ye* **shall** *receive them."* "All things" would not include collective things like health and happiness, but specific things, like rejuvenating a certain malfunctioning organ, or gaining the necessary inspiration to write a book such as this.

Jesus may have known all there is to know about quantum physics, but his audience did not (and still does not). So He choose words that would transcend—but not amend—science. Note the different tenses (bold face). He bids us first to believe a thing has already been accomplished, then its accomplishment will follow in the future.

This is a concise, precise direction for employing the power of thought by impressing on the universal subjective mind the particular thing which we desire as an already existing fact. In heeding this instruction we are thinking in the absolute which banishes all considerations or qualifying conditions (which suggest limitation and the prospect of adverse circumstances). This plants a seed internally that if left undisturbed, will germinate into external fruition. From this came the Process of Affirmation (what New Agers like to call the 'affie principle') that Norman Vincent Peale long ago packaged and labeled 'The Power Of Positive Thinking.'

For more insight into the workings of the mind/consciousness, turn to one of Christ's latterday interpreters

DEMYSTIFYING THE MYSTERY

As this is written, the mind as healer is coming out of occult closets into the mainstream, courtesy of PBS and Bill Moyers whose award-winning series, "Healing And The Mind" has made believers out of professional skeptics.

121

(circa 1900 A.D.), Thomas Troward, who found scientific method in Jesus' mysterious practices.

"All branches of physical science demonstrate the fact that every completed manifestation, of whatever kind and on whatever scale, is started by the establishment of a nucleus, infinitely small but endowed with an unquenchable energy of attraction, causing it to steadily increase in power and purpose, until the process of growth is completed and the matured form stands out as an accomplished fact. Now if this be the universal method of Nature, there is nothing unnatural in supposing that it must begin its operation at a stage further back than the formation of the material nucleus. That originating energy is Mind or Will."

"The action of the Mind plants that nucleus which, if allowed to grow undisturbed, will eventually attract to itself all the conditions necessary for its manifestation in outward visible form.

"Now the only action of Mind is Thought; and it is for this reason that by our thoughts we create corresponding external conditions.

Troward sums up his argument saying "The starting-point of all things is in thought-images or ideas, for no other action than the formation of such images can be conceived of spirit prior to its manifestation in matter. Therefore, *our thought of anything forms a spiritual prototype of it, thus constituting a nucleus or center of attraction for all conditions necessary to its eventual externalization by the law of growth inherent in the prototype itself.*

That's the good news.

If we try to hurry the working of the law and become anxious for the outcome, or employ wrong methods, or give up hope, we deny the germinating power of the seed we have planted. In either case, says Troward, "We are in effect forming a fresh spiritual prototype of an opposite character to our desire, which neutralizes the one first formed... thus evil is brought to us by precisely the same law as good. If we reverse the action of a cause we at the same time reverse the effect."

In other words, as a man thinketh ... so he is. For better or for ill.

There is no free lunch.

The passages quoted were excerpted from Troward's Edinburgh Lectures On Mental Science, presented in 1904, published in 1909. Given the dates, some of his scientific references might appear quaint, yet nowhere do his conclusions hang on theories that have since been discredited. Nor is the Holy Bible ("the most deeply occult of all books" says Troward) in disagreement but rather lays much stress upon the efficacy of faith and the destructive influence of unbelief.

The power of affirmation

Applying this wisdom is as simple as formulating the ideal conception of your desire; which is stated in the positive (without imposing conditions, alluding to a pre-existing 'problem' or 'lack of,' or otherwise insinuating anything negative).

Should you wish to escape the clutches of Demon Rum, for example, concoct an affirmation that puts you where you want to be—i.e., acknowledging the serenity of sobriety, being in control of your self, or any other perceived advantage to abstinence. Recite your affirmation many times upon rising and when retiring, and as often as possible in-between. Render it in writing and post in plain sight. Simple as that.

You don't have to understand the metaphysical Law of Attraction to harness your Mind Power. But because the process is indeed simple, and the condition to be produced is so far from your objective reality, one may be forgiven for at first feeling not only doubtful but downright silly while voicing their affirmation. The substance abuser who's going through the tortures of the damned while giving thanks for the opposite reality will have little faith that the outcome will be as envisioned. But by persisting, it will be accomplished.

When you wish to correct a condition that is causing you pain, the desired relief burdens the process with a sense of urgency. Relief cannot be scheduled, of course.

But your ability to bear the pain is supported by the knowledge it will pass in due time. You don't have to make-believe you believe the affirmation. *You only have to believe in believing.* That which you repeated by rote, as an exercise to begin with, will, at some point have become a reality. In hindsight, as it were.

Students of Mental Science find it easier to understand how the mind can influence the body with which it is so intimately associated, than how it can influence circumstances. Yet the action of thought-power (or indeed prayer, if you prefer that format) is not limited to circumscribed individuality. If your wishes are in line with the law of growth's everlasting forward/upward movement, there is nowhere in Nature any power to restrict the fulfillment of those wishes.

It is entirely within the province of Mental Science to wish for a home for your family. Not just the idea of a home, or a million dollar home on far-distant shores, but a specific house you are seeking to purchase. Besides creating an affirmation giving thanks for making this dream come true, and reciting it diligently despite a constant stream of difficulties with such as the financing, termites, appliances, ad nauseam, you visualize yourself living in it; cooking in it; making love in it; celebrating Christmas in it. Not what it would be like, but what it *is* like! See your furniture in it. Walk down its hall with your mind's eye. Brush your teeth in the bathroom. Do some landscaping. Chat with the neighbors. In the middle of one of those mental 'visits' you'll find it is in fact yours. Daydreaming is a powerful form of affirmation. If it's a certain job you want, or a job with a certain company, daydream about having it; reinforcing that daydream with a specific affirmation.

We don't always get what we want, of course. One cannot ask for the moon, or four eyes, or even Joan Collins. As Alice said in Wonderland, "You can't believe the impossible." The object of your desires must be attainable, do-able. The house you yearn for should be obtainable—i.e., for sale, at a price that is within the realm of the possible. Even when we correctly apply the principles outlined above we do not always receive what is asked. If, indeed, your method was efficacious, and you persisted without imposing deadlines or other conditions, and your affirmations was not confirmed—that likely will prove to be a blessing, albeit disguised in disappointment. That would be a clear sign your intention thwarted the law of growth, or, if you subscribe to the Hindu tantras, it crossed swords with your Karma. It's not even a question of being a Polly Anna; of it not being right for you, or of all the unseen troubles the denial saved you. It just couldn't have happened. It was an unreality. A nonevent. Forget it.

Doubting is dangerous to your health

None of the above is likely to satisfy those who take great pride in being rational; those people who are slaves to their senses, rejecting what they are unable to touch, see, hear, smell or hear. And verily, these are the people who must remain dependent on science to make the invisible visible; the unknowable knowable. And so science shall, but in the meantime, millions of these sense-oriented people are going to suffer unnecessarily.

NOTES TO MYSELF

CHAPTER XV

CHOICES

The Only Thing Worse Than a Bad Decision Is No Decision

The older we are, the more indecisive we become. A generality, but how many decisive 70-year old people do you know?

Even the most trivial choices—what to eat, what to wear, what video to rent—are agonized over, and over, and over. When it comes to making 'big' decisions, like whether to sell the old homestead and move to Golden Acres, most seniors end up sitting on the fence waiting for the winds of fate to blow them one way or the other.

This unwillingness to wrestle with the pros and cons of choice often precipitate crises requiring 'snap decisions.' Fence-sitters don't mind making those kinds of decisions because, by definition, a 'snap decision' leaves no time to weigh the pros and cons. Hence there's no responsibility for the outcome.

Another way we avoid confrontations with choice is to encapsulate ourselves in a predictable life-style, where every move is pre-scheduled, as in the Army, a cult, prison or some retirement community.

An age-old ploy

Those who can't afford life in a Leisure Village manage to limit their decision-making by becoming 'set in their ways.' By refusing to change their ways, the elderly are actually refusing to make the choices that change necessitates.

'Change' is the real culprit here, representing as it does the progression from young to old. Trying to maintain the status quo is just another way of denying the inevitable.

Another manifestation of indecisiveness is gullibility. It's not just coincidence that 'old folks' are the preferred prey of false prophets, pie-in-the-sky investment schemes and other bunko artists. The problem is not in *over* trusting someone else, or even *under* trusting one's own self. Rather it is avoiding responsibility. If your reading of the tea leaves leads you astray, you can blame Captain Lipton.

All this has nothing to do with senility, and everything to do with experience. Anyone who's been around for fifty, sixty or seventy years has had a lot of experience making bad decisions; all of them made for good reasons. That leads to the conclusion that the only way to avoid making a bad decision is to make no decision.

A misery of choice

Experience also has taught us there are at least a million ways to skin every cat. That knowledge creates 'a misery of choice.' It's never a simple matter of 'this' versus 'that.' You could spend the rest of your life comparing the pluses and minuses of various vacuum cleaners and still have no idea which make and model will best serve your purposes.

Innocence is bliss

When you were a kid, or even a young adult, you had no problem making up your mind ... about anything. You chose a mate and a career as easily as you now choose a sweater or decide on what movie to see. Youth isn't decisive as much as it is inexperienced. When that lack of experience leads to a bad experience, they are more than willing to forgive themselves and go merrily on their way, with a win-some/loose-some attitude. But when you find yourself on the plus side of fifty, time is not on your side.

The indecisiveness that haunts life's latter years is aided and abetted by a culture that permits, yea, encourages, the elderly to leave important decisions to those who are willing and eager to fill the decision-making vacuum: family, the health care industry and various private and public agencies that exist for that purpose. These surrogate decision-makers take the elderly's unwillingness to decide for themselves as indication they are unable to. And too many senior citizens are happy to foster that impression.

There are plenty of oldsters who shift for themselves in the middle of nowhere. When you're miles from any help, you help your self—no dithering over decisions.

People do what they have to do. When we are surrounded with social services, we're inclined to lean on them.

As understandable as it may be for people to become more indecisive with age, we must fight that inclination, for among other reasons, it petrifies our psyches and atrophies those functions that are inimical to human existence.

One of the psychological problems of aging is that it effectively reduces our options. The list of things we can no longer do or be grows with each passing year. So we should greet every decision with open arms because decisions require choice, and choice involves alternatives.

Every time we duck a decision, not only do we deny ourselves the luxury of options, but we forfeit our human prerogative. For one of the distinguishing characteristics of human life is choice making. Other forms of life don't make rational choices, or even irrational choices. They are driven, by instinct, to make the right choice. A rooster doesn't *decide* to cross the road. He has no choice but to cross because a cute little chicken is clucking on the other side.

The physics of life

We choose to live. On a macro level, hundreds of millions of choices enter our nervous systems every second. Were we to accept them all, we would be overwhelmed and die in utter confusion.

Our built-in bio-systems monitor and control the millions of incoming signals so that only a small number reach the brain, and even a lessor number are passed on to the seat of conscious awareness.

There is an analogy to be found in making a home recording. Your tape recorder picks up more background noise than we are consciously aware of at any given moment—i.e., the sounds of passing traffic, the ticking of a clock, barking dogs, a dishwasher, the hum of various other electrical appliances, to say nothing of radio and TV ... what Milton called "the dismal universal hiss." Our brain has learned to ignore what it deems extraneous to survival.

Living organisms, your self included, select, from the barrage of electromagnetic waves entering our individual environments, only those frequencies likely to contain beneficial or threatening information.

On the personal or micro level, choices are basic to free will. What we choose to think and do determines our human persona and the quality of our lives. Nothing good nor bad happens to you without your agreement, whether that agreement is consciously or unconsciously arrived at.

No place to hide

And make no mistake—when you choose not to choose you are not avoiding the issue. You merely are leaving the decision-making to unconscious mechanisms; hardly the way to raise your consciousness and take charge of your destiny.

There is no way you can avoid making certain decisions on demand. Every day is full of those. Like when you come to a fork in the road: either you turn left or you turn right. (Of course, you can choose not to choose and continue straight-ahead, thereby avoiding all future decisions!)

Most of these choices must be made instanter, with no opportunity for forethought. In that sense our decisions are more akin to reactions. It's when we have time to think about it that we get tied up in knots.

The lesson here is welcome every opportunity to choose.

And don't get all stressed out worrying about making the right decision. 'Right' in the short-run may prove 'wrong' in the long run. Conditions and circumstances change, making 'right' 'wrong' or vice versa. Foreseeing the future is, at best, a crap shoot. Nothing wrong with trying to peer ahead. But when it doesn't turn out as expected, don't be too quick to draw a line and call yourself 'wrong.' The movie isn't over till it's over. And even then, there's a sequel.

What's most important is stepping up to the plate and taking a swing, come what may. Just standing there, with the bat on your shoulder, is no way to play the game.

Many if not most decisions can be reduced to a choice between what you'd like to do versus what you 'should' do. Conventional wisdom usually dictates what 'should' be done.

And all too often that's at odds with what you'd like to do. When you do something you don't want to do, frequently it turns out 'wrong' either because you're not good at it or you more or less unconsciously resisted doing what's necessary to make it 'right.'

But when you follow your bliss it's much more likely to turn out 'right,' for among other reasons, it's easier to be successful doing what you like to do. Also, most every choice is involves pluses and minuses. When you go against your desires, the negative fallout is not easily forgiven. Whereas when you listen to your heart, you'll focus on the positive results and discount the minuses.

There's still another reason not to do what you 'should' do. 'Shoulds' always come from the outside, in the form of advice, laws, custom and convention. When it turns out wrong, the source of the 'shoulds' will be blamed, be that a real estate agent, stock broker, guru, Judeo-Christian ethics, Kiplinger Magazine or that no-good brother-in-law. This creates resentments. And as you read in Chapter five, that only makes matters worse. On the other hand, desires come from inside. When you follow your heart's desire, it's *your* heart and *your* desire. If you don't like where it led, count yourself lucky you have no one else to blame.

CHAPTER XVI

THE FUTURE IS NOT WHAT IT USED TO BE

ill the future ever arrive? ... Should we continue to look upwards? Is the light we can see in the sky one of those which will presently be extinguished?

—Victor Hugo

When we're young, with time to spare, there's little interest in The Future. Young people are NOW people, in the moment. The future is five or ten years hence. At twentysomething, fiftysomething is not on your list of things to think about.

It's a much different story when the passage of time foreshortens our futures. As the hourglass becomes bottom-heavy we start looking ahead, wondering what's around every next corner.

If The Future isn't yet a preoccupation with you, give it time. When sixty-five or seventy rolls around The Future will be running your life. That's what 'financial planning' is all about. And preventative health care. Isn't that why people sell a house on a hill with all those stairs—because, in a few years, they may not make it to the top.

So any book about 'successful aging' had best address this matter of The Future.

A future without end

This life—our present state of consciousness—will end with a new beginning. It would follow that our birth marked the end of an unknown or unremembered state of being. These beginnings and ends are best viewed as transitions; passing from one state to another, and so on through all eternity.

Granted, at fiftysomething people are more concerned with their immediate or tactical futures —i.e., the balance of this earthly existence. But in another fifteen or twenty years, chances are you'll be more concerned with the only future that remains: the everlasting future; the Great Beyond.

A future of a third kind

Then there is the future of our species: wither Homo Sapiens? What will become of The Family Of Man? Are we just one of Nature's passing fancies? Or are all her other fancies here to entertain and/or challenge us?

Be that as it may, all these futures are the subject of this chapter, starting with Mankind's destiny; a future that's already here. We can't experience it because we're stuck in that ol' time/space continuum. But we can put on our visionary glasses and preview some of the coming attractions.

To give you an idea of where your relatives will be a

couple of thousand years from now, put your self in the sandals of a Roman Legionnaire standing guard at Hadrian's Wall who suddenly is transported from 100 A.D. to today's Disney World.

Everything experienced by that time traveller no doubt would impress him as miraculous. Whereas, in fact, every 'miracle' he encountered would be a logical consequence of the universal laws in effect during Constantine's reign. The point being—a preview of 4,000 A.D. would boggle our minds in similar fashion. And yet whatever becomes possible 2,000 years hence, is possible here and now, given the know-how. Today's 'miracles' are tomorrow's science.

Most of Homo Sapiens' future progress will be in the Science Of Mind arena, whereby the mind gains dominion over matter.

The Law Of Growth

Before boggling your mind with the phenomenal future, there are a few things you need to know about the nature of Nature. One thing actually: *The effort of Nature is forever and always upward.* The purpose of this process is perpetual refinement.

This is the immutable evolutionary law of the universe. It applies to the sum of its parts and each of its parts—e.g., you.

The ultimate objective of this evolution, as it affects our terrestrial destiny, is towards what might be considered superhuman status; a kind of angelic being more plasmic or ethereal than opaque. (Lighter is brighter! The less dense we are, the less dense we are! and the more easily we can rise above terrestrial travails!) This radiant entity would seem to already have one foot in Heaven. However speculative this vision, Homo sapien's brief tenure on this whirling orb already offers epistomological and empirical evidence that we are being perfected. The refinement that began ever so slowly in the beginning, now seems to be gathering momentum, like the proverbial rolling snowball. What's true on the macro scale is true on the micro—i.e., all this applies to you, right here and right now. About which more follows.

But first consider how far we've come in just a few hundred, much less a few thousand years. Can you imagine a pack of Visagoths rallying to halt the slaughter of seal pups, or a bunch of Elizabethans protesting the cutting of a giant Sequoia, or ancient Romans rising up in righteous indignation over an unjust war?

Five centuries ago the great mass of humanity lived as peasants and slaves. It required dawn to dusk labor to half-fill their bellies. Survival left no time or desire to develop a higher consciousness, to wonder and reach for answers that didn't relate to food, sex and warmth. When the Industrial Revolution brought a degree of leisure time to the masses, people had time to think about thinking, which moved them closer to the angels on high and further from the beasts in the fields.

Homo sapien's evolution from bent-over beast to today's relative elegance is testimony that man, like Rome, wasn't built in a day... or even six days. With every generation we become more refined; a 'higher' form of being; more aware of our potential; more intent on reaching it. (The reader who would question this premise, based on all the brutal bashing going on around the globe and especially in our inner cities, might wish to turn now to the rear matter and there read "The Best Of Times, The Worst Of Times.")

Blue is new

Fifteen or twenty thousand years ago, primitive Aryans only perceived one color. Just five or six thousand years ago—a mere tick on the evolutionary clock—Indo-Europeans could not recognize the color blue. Aristotle spoke of the "tri-color rainbow;" Homer of the "wine-dark sea and rosy-tipped dawn." Democritus knew of no more than four colors—black, red, yellow and white. According to an exhaustive body of research performed in 1901 by Richard Bucke, M.D. (author of *Cosmic Consciousness*), in the ten thousand lines of the Rig Veda, the Zend Avesta and all the Homeric poems, the sky is described thousands of times without one mention of blue. That's because color sense is a recently acquired human faculty (with those colors in the blue spectrum being the most recently perceived) appearing in the race after the sense of shame and remorse.

This now-you-don't-see-it, now-you-do is just one more indication man is developing, being perfected. Not all of us are being perfected at the same rate, however.

141

Somebody had to recognize blue before somebody else. Blueness didn't just happen to everyone simultaneously —as if God declared blue to exist and splashed it across the sky one morning so everyone could look up and exclaim, "Hallelujah, it's blue." Because only a few eyes evolved to register blue before the many, early blue seers surely had trouble relating what they saw to their blue-blind friends. (Perhaps the first asylums were filled with folk who babbled about blue.)

A question of morality

Morality, evidently, is our most recently acquired faculty. Being new it is by no means pervasive. As a consequence, there are many amoral people—those folks who patently are devoid of morality—and many more who are partially moral, which is to say, frequently immoral.

An exceptional future

All this makes the point that what a few (wo)men have today, all (wo)men will have in due time. Today's exceptions will be tomorrow's rule.

Certainly there are no lack of such exceptions to inspire us. All manner of quasi sciences and unexplained extrasensory phenomena provide a hint of things to come.

In China they remove tubercular lungs and other damaged organs without any kind of anesthesia, only one thin needle inserted in the right forearm. Afterwards, the patients sit up and dress without a wince. What's more, Kirlian photography which records the aura-producing life force or field of energy surrounding our bodies has shown that the strongest flares which shine out of the skin like searchlights match the traditional acupuncture points. Using Kirlian 'blueprints', the Russians have produced an electronic device, the 'Tobiscope,' to mark the points on a patient's body. Guided by this means, holistic practitioners are producing dramatic cures using needles, electricity and sound waves to stimulate the key points. The object is balance; bringing the *Yin* and *Yang* into equilibrium, thereby allowing *Chi* (the life force) to circulate unimpeded. The *Tai Chi* discipline employs the same principle, as a form of preventative medicine, enabling its elderly devotees to (re)gain the vitality of youth.

Eyes in your ears and other phenomena
Blind people have been able to 'see' with the tip of their fingers, the end of their nose or an ear lobe.

Masters of various occult arts can send their electromagnetic energy (or *Chi*), in concentrated form, outside the body, whether to move inanimate objects or to affect the movement of other human bodies. Sometimes this power to move energy outside the body is possessed involuntarily, much to the consternation of the possessor. One such woman was persuaded to demonstrate her power to move objects by force of will in a laboratory (controlled!) environment. In one instance she caused a slice of bread to move across a table and into her open mouth. Another time she was able to separate an egg yolk from the white and agitate either part separately, all at arm's length. It was determined she had an abnormal electrostatic field, an unusual brain-wave pattern that during the experiments generated fifty-times more voltage. Her body rhythms seemed to produce a beat that was picked up and amplified by the field around her producing a magnetic effect, causing the object she focused on to be attracted to her or repelled from her.

Psychokinesis (PK) experiments have been conducted over the years by a multitude of reputable scientific institutions. At Duke University they devised an electronic coin 'flipper' to eliminate the human factor in an experiment to test the force of will on games of chance. In 32,000 'flips' the subjects controlled the outcome with odds of ten million to one against chance. In Germany, a 17-year old schoolboy tossed a coin 10,000 times and was able to affect its fall with results that had odds of a billion to one against chance. PK has caused a compass needle to rotate like a watch's second hand. And despite the diminishing effect distance has on force fields, PK is not effected by separation.

Telepathy, the ability to transmit messages/images via brain waves over long distances and through water, is by now a well-established fact.

Thoughtography is another unexplained phenomena whereby the subject can produce recognizable images of distant objects just by imagining them while staring into a camera.

Healing hands and green thumbs

As mentioned in a previous chapter, it has been proved beyond a scientific doubt that some Healers' hands really do heal. And contrariwise, a negative result also can be reproduced.

Similarly, it has been repeatedly demonstrated that some gardeners actually generate an energy field that has a beneficial effect on plant growth.

Precognition, knowing in advance, identifies a cluster of occult arts, including divination, the *I Ching*, Tarot, consulting oracles (including your neighborhood psychoanalyst). These 'phenomena' all have to do with expanding our present potential more than with forecasting the future.

The mind of Ancient Man was able to gain dominion over matter by clinging to rituals and behavioral patterns that unleashed unseen forces or waves of energy capable of cutting stone, lifting and even destroying objects. Low-frequency sound waves focused on a building miles away can knock it down as effectively as a major earthquake.

The mind can condition the body's heart rate, blood pressure, and just about every other bodily function. In yoga, Zen, and some African cults, digestion, metabolism, kidney function and body temperature can be reduced to that of an hibernating animal, considered to be lethal for a 'normal' man. As covered elsewhere, it can make warts appear and disappear. In Tibet, the practice of *Lung-gom* produces the ability to travel very rapidly across some of the earth's highest and most inhospitable terrain. These adepts do not run but seem to lift themselves from the ground, proceeding by leaps, covering over 300 miles in less than thirty hours. [By comparison, marathon runners take more than two hours to travel 24 miles on good roads at sea level.] Another Tibetan disciple is *tumo*, an ability to combat cold in a country that is almost entirely 10,000 feet above sea level. When *tumo* training is complete, students are tested on a windy winter night by wrapping them in a sheet that's been dipped into a river through a hole in the ice and has to be completely dried by body heat at least three times during the night. After qualification, the adept will only wear a single cotton garment in all seasons and at any height. Several Everest expeditions have reported seeing completely naked hermits living above the permanent snow line.

Shamans and crop circles

Autosuggestion not only alters bodily functions for the good, it can kill. Thousands die every year at the hands of their unconscious. People who believe they've been bewitched 'think' themselves into illness or death, the victim being the source of the 'supernatural' power, not the witch doctor. But you don't necessarily have to think destructively to suffer the effects of another's malevolence. Shamans can induce choking in an unaware victim miles away. Gloom and fear can be passed from mind to mind without being face to face.

And pray tell, what manner of intelligence is creating

those increasingly intricate geometric crop circles (not to be confused with the crop of man-made hoaxes)? We may never know their source or their purpose. But we do know this: Whether they're signals from outer space or the signature of hovering extraterrestrials, there is no force available to other worlds that is not available to this world. Their physics are our physics. Matter/energy is the same throughout the universe. While other life forms from other dimensions may be better able to harness this universal potential, evidence of such accomplishments should inspire rather than frighten and mystify us.

For the most part, we know how autosuggestion, PK, hypnosis, et alia works. We have yet to discover why, the mode and method.

Clearly, the mind has the capacity to consciously alter 'normal' processes, producing effects that appear miraculous to the layman. But rather than abrogating the laws of physics, the mental function appropriates natural forces, albeit in ways we do not understand. Yet.

We know ritualized magic produces hallucinations, the same way lack of sleep does. The ritual, like the effects of deprivation, produces the reaction. Telepathy and meditation are enhanced by lowering the acidity in blood, which produces a rise in carbon-dioxide pressure in the lungs and a reduction of oxygen reaching the brain. A vegetarian diet and high altitude produces these same results. Consequently, people who practice meditation observe strict dietary rules, and yogis prefer the mountains.

All these phenomena impress as mysterious because seemingly invisible mental forces are effecting visible objects. More mysterious yet, we don't know what it all means. Why did these transcendent capacities evolve in the first place? What is their biological function? They are not needed for survival. Clearly, our mental potential far exceeds our materialistic needs. After everyone's well fed, clothed and sheltered—what then?

ROOM FOR IMPROVEMENT

Computers are built with excess capacity; to accommodate future circuitry in much the same fashion our brain is equipped with 'expansion slots.' Like the computer maker who provides this extra built-in capacity with no idea of how it will be utilized, our maker may be leaving it to us to fill our mental capacity as we think proper.

Might not these 'supernatural' powers be a portent of things to come; the tools of a higher type man and woman; one who lives in a four-dimensional world?

The difference between contemporary humans and future humans will be a difference in consciousness—between *individual consciousness,* and *universal consciousness,* an awareness of the self as an integral part of the universal whole, as a grain of sand is to a beach.

The millennium previewed

That is what we are coming to (if we don't destroy our terrestrial base in the process of getting there). The changes this universal or cosmic consciousness will make in our inner life will change totally the outer life. We will not see others of our kind as competitive threats and those unfortunate traits we now ascribe to 'human nature' no longer will condemn us to repeating the sins of our fathers. Indeed, the world dominated by people possessing cosmic consciousness will be as far removed from the world of today as this is from the world as it was before the advent of self-consciousness.

This is not to suggest you are a mere stepping stone along the path to this earthly perfection. Humankind will attain the status of demigods only by the *conscious* effort of each individual to refine him or herself.

Although a one-by-one, step-by-step evolutionary process, it will take much less time to get from here to there than it has taken us to reach this halfway point. If our momentum does not encounter any brick walls.

> "Your individual actions may seem unimportant, but it is absolutely essential you do them."
> —Gandhi

> "Nobody made a greater mistake than he who did nothing because he could only do a little."
> —Edmund Burke

Nor does the process of refinement mean all men and women are moving higher at the same rate, if at all. Indeed not. It is quite obvious that cultural conditions consign some of us to conditions that chain the consciousness to a physical, sense-dominated existence. But as morality and compassion become integrated into human nature, those who lead the way will not be content to let 'the devil take the hindmost.' The gaps now separating people will be narrowed and finally eliminated.

While certain faculties like color sense, evolve without the individual's willful effort, the New Consciousness will not come to those who do not seek it. Those who do will be much better equipped to succeed, while those who don't will be better equipped to fail.

In the meantime ... there you are, a man or woman, struggling to find your 'center' in this the September of your years, during the waning moments of the 20th Century A.D. Is there a message here for you?

Yes, indeed.

The way of least resistance

It behooves each of us to obey the highest within us. To resist is to interfere with Nature's upward effort; a useless and painful endeavor.

The high road is the right road because that is the way of contentment, good health, harmonious relationships and successful undertakings. While the low road is pebbled with pain and conflict; fruitless effort and disappointment.

The physical forces unleashed by The Creator's original thought operate by rules that punish anything that impedes Nature's upward effort. Thus lies, hate, wanton lust and violence are downers. Dark emotions disturb your God-given vibrational frequencies causing psychic and physical disorders. Love and compassion, on the other hand, are uppers; emotions that raise our consciousness and keep it in sync with the cosmic pulse. (Do not, dear reader, allow language to interfere with the *idea* being expressed. Words like 'God' and 'Nature,' 'psychic,' 'cosmic' and 'vibrational frequencies' may be, for some, emotionally-charged, causing your mind to wander from the idea. For more about the inadequacy of language to convey transcendent ideas, refer to "Beyond Words" in the rear matter.)

Looking beyond the mortal plane, the soul takes with it what it gained here: the sum total of all your thoughts and deeds. A lifetime spent entertaining the senses leaves the subjective or spiritual mind atrophying in darkness with no idea of itself. When the senses cease to function, the consciousness remains earthbound, unable to function on its own. Some might call that state Limbo, Purgatory or just plain Hell. Whatever it is, it's a spiritual No-Man's Land to be avoided at all costs.

The bottom line

Now is the time to give your spiritual consciousness flying lessons. This does not require you to retreat to a religious cloister any more than it excludes pleasures of the flesh. It's more a matter of emphasis having to do with the friends you keep, the books you read, the music you hear, the thoughts you think.

Food for thought

Feed your consciousness quality thoughts. For just as physical health depends on what fuel is fed your body; the condition of your consciousness depends on what you feed the mind. Garbage in, garbage out.

If the inner you has been starved, or stuffed with a lot of junk, a new diet might be in order.

If not now, when?

CHAPTER XVII

LETTING GO

*It Is No Use To Cling To Rocks
That Are Falling With You.*
—Alan Watts

Despite all the foregoing, would it be fair to say you're not exactly thrilled to be fiftysomething? All things considered, wouldn't you like to turn back the clock to somewhere around thirtysomething?

The next question is why? The answer to that most probably would be something like, "Because everything is new and still possible at that age," or some other euphemism for 'young.'

Since time immemorial, 'young' has always been preferable to 'old.'

Not that you're exactly moldy at fiftysomething. Call it 'getting old,' or, if you prefer—the latter stages of 'middle-age.' Whatever fiftysomething is, 'young' is better, right?

O' sure, you may be the exception—one of those people suffering from a kind of reverse denial who insist they're well rid of all the trials and tribulations connected to youth. But try as you might to put a happy face on that wan and weathered visage in the mirror, deep down where your fears rumble, you'd trade the present for the past. Admit it.

Even after all this posturing, you still haven't explained the real reason you aren't happy about being fiftysomething. Nobody ever admits to the real reason 'young' is better than 'old.' We spend our lives beating around the bush that hides the Grim Reaper.

Okay, now that it's out in the open, let's face up to the subject. Not that death and dying are high on your list of things to worry about right now. That's exactly why this is the right time to gain some sort of insight into the state of being that exists when the consciousness is allowed to seek its proper level, free of form. Given that, you can walk tall into the sunset without faking it. And better concentrate on the business of living in the here-and-now in the meantime.

Those who are prepared for the transition are better able to avoid the confusion and terror that awaits the disoriented soul. This isn't something to be left to the last minute. Your consciousness level before it separates from the body determines the level your consciousness will seek when it begins to roam the spiritual plane.

Gandhi was ready

Like Jesus, Gandhi was well-prepared to meet his maker. You will recall he stepped out to give a press conference and received four bullets for his trouble. As he fell over dead, Gandhi called out, "Ram," the Hindu word for God. That's being ready! He didn't have to remember to say it. Ram was right there at the center of his consciousness; on the tip of his tongue, ready when needed. Instead of saying, "Ughh!" or "Good-bye" or "Forgive them" in that traumatic instant, Gandhi goes out riding a wavelength that will take him straight to his reward. Impressive. And inspirational.

All of which recommends the upcoming decade, when sensory distractions are on the wane, as a good time to get your spiritual consciousness in shape for that unique event. (Birth being the only other experience that rivals death.)

The process of elimination

The training regime recommended by spiritual mentors, both east and west, would put Weight Watchers to shame. We are exhorted to shed all those attachments that puff up the ego and delight the senses. The idea being, when the body is dropped, the consciousness will find it difficult to operate independently if it's attached to desires only a body can fulfill. Poltergeists and ghosts, incidentally, are beings stuck on a low, in-between (astral) plane trying to get back into a body —by 'taking over' a body— to regain their only source of pleasure, be that power, sex or whatever. The only bodies they can possess, reportedly, are those possessed by the same needs. Something to think about, that!

Some attachments, including many of those we are born with—such as the urge to merge and feed our face—

> "Every year I try to simplify, to give up something (else): The big house and yard; the country club; booze; the Sunday TIMES".
>
> —Whit Hobbs

fall away at the other end of life without any effort on our part; it's Nature's benevolent way. Those attachments we acquire along life's path, especially attachments that sustain an inflated ego, are not shed with age. Someone addicted to power is not likely to loose that lust later in life. Even when the source of their power is lost—be it sex, wealth or political position—the desire to wield it is not. They are consigned to live their later years in a state of frustration.

Among the list of attachments you are better off without is the attachment to who you think you are. Your adopted role. Whatever that is—an architect, professor, lover, athlete, mother—you are not likely to remain that to the end of your life, much less in your after life. So don't get too attached to your role in life in order to make it easier to let go of it later in life.

There is no attachment that will compromise the next twenty or thirty years of your life as much as an attachment to time. What's so insidious about this attachment is that it increases with age. This goes beyond the survival instinct that Nature installed to insure we would live long enough to pass on critical information to our progeny. When well past that point, we're still hanging on for dear life notwithstanding all the promises about Happy Hunting Grounds. Here, again, we desire that what isn't or can't be. The less we have (of time), the more we want. As time runs out, the more precious it becomes to us, the more we try to hoard it.

Tired of living and scared of dying

The attachment to time is really an attachment to our physical self, to our senses. We cling to our body even when it is no longer entertained by rich food, sweet smells, and erotic images. Those who are tired of living but more scared of dying need a better understanding about the nature of sense-less existence. (The closest approximation of that would be the so-called sensory deprivation experience produced by suspending yourself in a flotation tank: when deprived of physical sensation you are left with only realizations.) This is not something that can be accomplished (snap!) like that. But a good place to begin is to realize you've got nothing to loose. It's just a transformation of energy. Thinking you're more than that, and will loose that, is what's frightening.

The Pharaohs and other ancient aristocrats tried to take the 'good life' with them. Think of the time that was wasted in that endeavor, to say nothing of the lives that were lost constructing their Heavenly capsules. The consciousness needs no help from the material world in order to seek its proper place in the more rarefied, spiritual atmosphere. That doesn't mean our consciousness can't become earth-bound.

Buddhists are given to banging gongs to encourage the deceased's departure from these familiar haunts. If the ego has kept the consciousness imprisoned in form with no idea of itself, when that form is dissolved, the consciousness is left homeless. According to the Tibetan Book Of The Dead, when we are unaware of any existence outside of form, the consciousness wanders lost in space, full of confusion, horror and panic.

Being handcuffed to time and form compromises not only the transformation of consciousness after it separates from the body; it prevents us from using this lifetime to best advantage. Instead of flowing with time as it streams by your consciousness, we try to stop it, dam it up, as if we could save some for later. Every minute you watch the clock is a minute wasted.

Like all value judgments, this is a matter of degrees. It is entirely fitting and perfectly proper to value time, especially at this time of life. This produces priorities: what's important and what's not. But when most of your time is spent worrying about the loss of time, trying to reverse the aging process, that's an extreme to be avoided. Again, because it patently is a waste of time, contributing nothing to the present moment.

Attachments of a third kind
The attachment to time and space leads to a whole panoply of desires that are connected to our body, and its taskmaster, the ego. As long as we are in control of these desires they're considered 'healthy.' When they start controlling us they're considered compulsions or addictions.

Addictions jerk us around something awful. Addictions compel us to harm ourselves as well as others, including loved ones.

Addiction is the worst kind of slavery. You volunteer for this form of enslavement. And your master is an inanimate object that can show no pity or remorse.

Breaking the chain that binds

Escaping the clutches of tobacco, alcohol and all the other physical compulsions that control us should be as easy as simply walking away from them. Actually it is easier than that. All you have to do is ... nothing. No thing.

Hanging-on to these attachments is what takes effort.

Alcoholics have to find the money, go out and buy the stuff, pour it, drink it, hide it, lie about it, ad nauseam ... all of which takes a lot of doing. And that's nothing compared to what we put ourselves through to fulfill some of our other passions.

Why is it we're willing to go to such great lengths to do something or be something that we'd be better off not doing or being?

The answer to that conundrum is not to be found in our desires as much as in the nature of desiring, whether its physical or psychological. Before you can be free of desire you must know you're caught. Once that's recognized, there are any number of ways to set your self free. That can involve checking into a recovery clinic or attending 12-step programs. Or doing it yourself, cold turkey. This usually takes the form of a frontal assault: confronting the object of your desire, then denying you desire it. If the desire for rich food is your problem, place a bit of pastry on a dish in front of you and keep yourself busy for an hour or two not eating it. There are more pleasant ways to spend an afternoon.

A more effective way of letting-go of your desires is by disassociation. You aren't desire. It's your body that does the desiring, prodded by a piggish ego. The disassociation strategy calls for separating the conscious self from the sentient self's desires.

Disassociate with the enjoyer

Whenever you catch your self giving in to an undesirable desire, become a witness. 'Witnessing' is not judgmental. It doesn't scold. Witnessing is simply observing, dispassionately, what's happening. Usually the only voice you hear is that of the enjoyer, or superego, which tries to compensate for the indulgence by assigning blame. "There I go again, giving in to my appetite—I'm hopeless." That's nothing but a cop-out. You've not only given in to the forbidden desire, but belittled your self in the process, which sets the scene for future indulgences.

Instead of listening to the enjoyer, make a conscious effort to become the witnesser who observes, "Here I am, eating pastry ..." This requires conscious effort, but the more time you spend witnessing, the more you disassociate your self from enjoying. You can't remain unconscious of your actions when you're consciously witnessing them. In time it will become a subliminal response. The process works for any kind of attachment, "Ah, yes—there's the desire for you-name-it ." Like any process, at first it will seem a silly waste of time.

Desires define your universe by affecting your perceptions. When a hungry person walks down a street, he only notices bakeries. When a pickpocket meets a saint, all he sees are pockets.

But when you persist and become more and more a witness, those attachments will just shrivel up and disappear from your screen.

Try not thinking of purple elephants

Desires are illusive things. Confronting them head-on is no way to deny them ... like if you try not to think of sex you become preoccupied with it. To diminish its influence you have to disassociate your self from the experience and thereby care less. Witnessing does that.

It's a valuable adjunct to the purification process: eliminating that which is unnecessary or interferes with Nature's upward effort.

And, to reconnect to this chapter's opening paragraphs—when you're rid of the body's desires you won't be so all-fired attached to your body, making it easier to bid it "Adieu."

The Hindus believe we keep coming back (whether to this or other places), in new and different forms, to work out our individual Karma—the idea being it takes many more than one incarnation to experience away all our desires or attachments. The ability of some people to recall past lives is given as testimony of this belief.

To be or not to be

However this process of elimination occurs, it seems the great cosmic dance of purification will not conclude until there are no more dancers. The ultimate destiny of all beings, known and unknown, is to become non-beings: to loose that which keeps us separate and apart from our maker.

Do not dismay. The objective is ecstasy, not oblivion.

The purpose of this existence, and any that may have preceded it, as well as what may follow, is to shed the attachments that are the indicia of individuality. When finally rid of the last one—the desire to be desire-less—we can merge with our maker, becoming one with the original 'One,' what amounts to a state of non-being, the ultimate act of letting-go.

LETTING GO

NOTES TO MYSELF

CHAPTER XVIII

THAT MANY-SPLENDORED THING

Some of its Splendors Are More Splendiforous Than Others

Of all the emotions known to man (and woman), none is more misunderstood, underrated and abused as that feeling we are wont to call 'love.' It is, at once, a universal emotion and rare as hen's teeth on Juan Fernandez Island.

Nine-hundred and ninety times out of a thousand it is used to describe sexual attraction and infatuation which are nothing more nor less than physiological and bio-chemical reactions Nature planted in our genes to insure the survival of the species. (Nothing wrong with that, but neither is it anything to wax poetic over.)

Physical attractions sometimes mature into affection (and its corollaries, empathy and kinship), a more be-nevolent emotion that relates to another person's per-sonality or inner qualities versus their outer measurements. Both romantic love and affection are di-rected at another object, usually animate, and become breeding grounds for all manner of psychodynamic dra-mas involving jealousy, hate and possessiveness, three of the most destructive and debilitating emotions known to (wo)man.

Another relationship we call love is the sharing of

loneliness. In a society that lacks the experience of community, many individuals share their lives not out of love but to relieve a sense of apartness; to avoid disintegration.

The highest form of romantic love—what Rollo May refers to as mature love—is an affirmation of the value and worth of the other person. To be capable of giving and receiving this, one needs be a fulfilled personality; a person in one's own right—having the capacity for independence. Whereas love of a more common type involves dependence.

This capacity for independence pre-supposes freedom. Certainly love not freely given is not love. Thus the highest form of romantic love is quite different from loving one's mother or child. The bond between family members often produces clinging; dependence. 'Giving' is often an expression of duty or responsibility.

Another common misconception is that love requires self-abnegation, 'giving up.' This leads our society to connect love to weakness—i.e., the weaker people are, the more they love; the stronger we are the less need to love. No wonder 'tenderness' has come to be linked with 'meek' and 'weak' (while in fact tenderness goes with strength!).

The reader may ask, "does not one lose oneself in love?" While true love involves merging one with the other, this coming together does not involve loss but amounts to a union (same as experienced during mutual orgasm). The act of merging is synergistic: the sum produced being greater than its parts.

We often use 'love' to describe a different kind of ardor. There is love of symbols like flags and crosses; thrones and other man-made institutions. These are closely allied with love of country, love of Lenin, love of Elizabeth Rex, love of Christ, Mohammed, Buddha, et al. More damage is done in the name of these loves than all the plagues, famines and natural disasters ever visited on this planet.

Love that wine

Some of us claim to love a certain vintage, cuisine, make and model car, music, activity, movie, a company or other affiliations, like the Masons, or an alma mater and even athletic

True love doesn't bind; it frees.

teams. Like romantic love, all these kinds of love are object-oriented and more or less conditionally awarded. If the 49ers have a loosing season, you will likely withhold your love. If your company fires you, you'll probably withdraw your allegiance. When your country fights an unjust war, you may lower the flag. When the opposite sex looses her shape or his erection, you are programmed to seek another to drool over.

At fiftysomething, you are not exempt from any of these possessive forms of love. But there will come a time, a few years hence, when you no longer will be victimized by your sexual appetite. (You'll relish sexual contact, as a side dish instead of hungering for it as the main dish.) Nor will you feel called on to place a constant stream of fresh conquests on your ego's alter. The prospect is not for a life without love, however. As your possessive period passes you can better experience not only familial love but a whole new level of love; higher-minded and more purifying than affirmative love between two individuals.

God is love

You are in love's inner sanctum when you *become* love. When you *are* love. Different than lover or loved, and loving.

When you are love, everyone around you is loved, every person you come in contact with is your lover — they experience your electromagnetic vibrations. If they are tuned to your frequency there's a harmonic convergence; they, too, for the moment, become love, and you are engulfed in an ocean of love. That's what Christ's love was/is about.

This is the highest form of love because it has no object but the experience or realization of love itself. There is no person or thing to possess. No conditions qualify it. It is ego-less; self-less. No harm is produced in the name of this love. It is a divine state. Something close to bliss and ecstasy. If the other forms of love keep you in the moment, give life meaning, make you feel so gosh-darned great — you ain't felt nothin' yet!

"Love is the key to all knowledge, wisdom and power. Dwell deep in this love and you will see as God sees."
— Christ In You

The reason *being* love is so transcendent and transforming may be explained in the energy or vibrational frequencies this love produces. There is nothing mysterious or mystical at work here. This a very real condition; it can be measured or tested, in the same way radio or brain waves register their presence.

All kinds of good flows from *being* love. You feel good and look radiant. All those around you bask in the reflected glory. You like everything, and everything likes you. It is also a state of grace; a state of consciousness in tune with the self-evolving, all-generating creative spirit we know as God/Allah/Jehovah/Creator/Unified Theory.

You are not love because you love God. Without demeaning reverence, that, too, is a form of selfish, conditional love whose object is reward and which separates you from what is being loved. You become love because of the sum total of all your thoughts and actions.

> "Peace can only be made by those who are peaceful, and love can only be shown by those who love."
> —Alan Watts

It is safe to say few mortals have attained this level of love in the absolute. Many aspire to and eventually will, but not as earth-bound beings, with all the impediments the human senses must deal with. If there are exceptions, they probably reside in monasteries or other cloisters far from the distractions the rest of us are so much in love with.

But that doesn't mean it is of no use to try as best you can to attain this state of love; to become it. It is neither useless nor fruitless. All our efforts over the millennia to become so have lifted us out of the primordial swamps to our present half-animal, half-divine state of being. It is all part of Nature's upward effort; the process of refinement. The desire to be love, to be engulfed in its divine embrace, puts you on the high road and keeps you there. By degrees your consciousness level will rise, and each degree moves you closer to the ideal.

The older you are, the easier it should be to stop loving (possessing) other objects and start loving love. In so doing, you will be in a state of grace having filled all the prescriptions offered in all the sacred books ever written. Nothing more is needed.

Nothing more is asked.

NOTES TO MYSELF

EPILOGUE

The End of the Beginning

That Churchillian phrase, delivered at the end of the Battle Of Britain to mark the beginning of the battle for Europe, is a most appropriate beginning for this ending. It is a reminder that fiftysomething is not the beginning of the end, but only the end of the beginning.

As you may recall, this book began with the acknowledgement the next two or three decades can be the most confining and monochromatic years of your life, or the most expansive and colorful. It all depends on the attitude you adopt in your fifties.

All that followed was calculated to install the 'right' attitude re: the (ir)relevance of chronological age; relieving your self of resentments and regrets; taking your parent's place at the edge; moving between objective and subjective realities and why the latter is a refuge for weary warriors retreating from the former; the problem with problems and how to make less of more; a technique for making the rest of your life an endless series of beginnings; avoiding the 'Inertia Syndrome,' that fossilizing process caused by a lack of challenge; a sampler of unconventional wisdom on the subject of your health; facing a miraculous future, and letting-go of what holds you down.

What effect all this may have on your attitude, only time and you can tell. If your hour-glass looked half-empty at the beginning and half-full to end with, the trees these pages were printed on will not have died in vain.

THE END OF THE BEGINNING

NOTES TO MYSELF

MOPPING UP

ODDS & ENDS
TOO SHORT TO BE CHAPTERS;
TOO GOOD TO BE DISCARDED

NOW VERSUS THEN

With age comes perspective. At fiftysomething you've seen enough to make comparisons, whether about the weather, politics or the latest fashions. This presents you with an advantage, one of the few, over Johnny Come Latelies. *You've been where they are at, as well as where they're going.* And you are not the least bit hesitate to employ this advantage at every opportunity. No matter that those with the most to gain from your observations are bound to ignore your input. And who can blame them. Every comparison you are wont to make is calculated to draw invidious comparisons between their 'now' and your 'then.' Your 'good ol' days,' be they ever so seedy, are seen to be at once "better" and "tougher" than the present day. This judgement is calculated to minimize the younger person's successes ("It never used to be so easy...") and maximize failures ("If you think times are tough now, you should have been around when ...").

In fact, there is never any real basis for comparing 'now' to 'then.' Every 'now' is one-of-a-kind. But that won't stop today's thirty-year olds from playing the same game twenty years from today!

AGE AND THE AGES

As the years pile up, our hindsight extends back beyond those 'The Good Ol' Days.' Patriarchs see themselves as participants in an Age or Epoch, a bundle of years lashed together with some significant common denominator. From this Olympian vantage point we can make comparisons on a much grander scale. Whereas the fifty year old is given to comparing the 1990s to the 1950s, septuagenarians are wont to relate 'The Atomic Age' to 'The Industrial Revolution.'

This appears to be a relatively new conceit. History offers little evidence our forbearers spent any time comparing their present with some dim dark past. To do so requires knowing where you're at. It also presumes history will see it the same way. No where is it indicated Michelangelo recognized himself as a Renaissance man, or that Shakespeare acknowledged he was living through the Elizabethan Age. It's only lately we rush to judgement re naming our own epoch. In doing so, we may be prematurely exiting a still extant age. Already that's led to 'turf wars.' Atomic scientists are inclined to memorialize their contributions, calling this the Atomic Age. Electronic engineers are wont to do likewise. And, no doubt, the people involved in the Biotech industry will wish to affix their own imprimatur to this chapter of the human drama. What future historians will call our time remains to be seen. Maybe 'The Nowhere Age.' In the meantime let's resist the temptation to anticipate their verdict.

WHY THE BEST OF TIMES ARE THE WORST OF TIMES

Now that you've reached a Senior position in our society, you can't help but feel a little responsible for these Life & Times. You certainly don't want to leave your fingerprints on an embarrassing page of history, much less the last page!

It is only human to consider the present an improvement over the past, if not the best of all possible worlds.

But even the most optimistic reviewer of the last 50 years is unlikely to issue a glowing report of our progress. Every time we seem headed in the right direction, along comes a Hitler, a man-made plague or some other unnatural disaster that derails our progress.

> Anyone who knew much about the past must conclude that the present was plainly better.
> —Thos. Babington Macaulay

"What a piece of work is man." Our silos bulge with surplus wheat while millions go without a crust of bread between them. Our buildings reach for the stars oblivious of the homeless huddled on their thresholds. We have one foot in Heaven, the other in Hell. One hand holds an olive branch, the other wears brass knuckles. Is this the future; the sum of the past?

It is always darkest before the dawn
One of the definitive characteristics of this Day & Age is the noise level. Today's victims do not suffer in

179

silence. The chorus of complaint has never been louder. And while we may tire of the endless keening, there is hope to be found in the protests.

In the dingy Dark Ages people didn't go around bitching about "these terrible times." People didn't expect anything but what they got: hunger, disease, misery, hopelessness.

Today we expect such a lot. We expect to work a little and earn mucho. We expect never to go hungry, never to be treated unjustly, to be well educated and well housed. Not that everyone is, but everyone expects it— thanks to the movies, TV, jet travel, satellite communications, FAX machines, modems and office-seeking politicians.

Our expectations also are a product of mankind's stunning progress from brute to our present state of being. As Heaven On Earth becomes conceivable, anything less is 1) noticed, and 2) resented. So we are rightly upset when some tinhorn generalissimo tortures a few of his disloyal subjects. But no such hue and cry would have been raised just fifty years ago. Fifty years ago few would know about it, and fewer still would raise a stink.

John Lennon was right back in '67 when he wrote, " ... it's getting bettah, getting bettah all the time ..." And the more we expect, the bettah it will get!

Walking vs. running

There are many who say we are trying to progress too fast; to redress too many grievances too soon. Blacks,

Chicanos, Haitians, Palestinians, Armenians, Azerbaijanis, Croats, Serbs, Somalis, Vietnam vets, American indians, transvestites, et al, are shouting, pushing and shoving to get their due and complaining bitterly when it is denied them. So we get the idea that there is so much—maybe more than ever—injustice around us, so many wrongs that need righting.

Yet the fact is—never has there been more effort to help the helpless, with all kinds of positive results to show for it. Indians are given back their homelands. Cubans are given refuge. Minorities are receiving a much better education. Women are getting equal access if not equal pay. Cross-dressers are donning military regalia. The light of world opinion makes it increasingly difficult to repress human rights. There is much left to be done, God knows. But it is happening — now more than ever, faster than ever.

It's as if humanity for centuries had been feeling its way through a pitch-black tunnel; every inch an agony. Only some inner spark lighted any hope and pushed one foot ahead of the other. Now, suddenly, a point of light is seen shining up ahead. The end of the tunnel is in sight!

Do you think so much humanity so long a prisoner to the dark will be content to continue shuffling slowly towards the light and freedom? Hell, no! A roar goes up, and everyone stampedes for the exits.

And those who have been in charge of mankind's groping progress find their orders, threats and entreaties now have little effect. They are ignored, derided, and run-over. That's because they are no longer needed to lead the way. Now people see where they want to go. They also see that their old warders—the generals, presidents, industrialists, bankers, policemen, even ministers—stand between them and their expectations. Trouble is, the Old Guard is operating with its back to the future. They don't see the light. To them it appears that people have lost their minds, rushing ahead wildly, trampling the laggard, shouting "Gimme," "Gimme," "Gimme."

No doubt about it: the first taste of freedom causes people to act precipitously. *Prison breaks are not exactly an orderly process.* Witness the fate of African Republics; the hullabaloo in Mother Russia; the bashing in the Balkans.

Those who witness the mayhem behind white picket fences are given to a lot of tsk-tsking about the way outstretched hands turn to fists. Sure, minorities have more rights than they did a hundred years ago, but they want even more—a predictable reaction to success, and a sure sign things are getting bettah all the time.

THERE'S NO PLACE LIKE HOME

where the feet may part
but not the heart;
the chain may lengthen
but n'er parts.

Being a social animal, (wo)man needs someplace to call home, be it e'er so humble. Without a cave or cottage to retreat to, we loose our bearings, become disoriented and irresponsible.

As we begin to loose our leaves, this need for a den or cloister grows into something even more basic. Come the moment of our greatest vulnerability, there's no place like home, especially if family and friends will be found there.

And yet too many—more each year—spend their last years as a 'guest,' ofttimes uninvited and unwelcome. If that last resort is an institution, woe be unto the institutionalized. This is no fit departure point. But given the economic realities, there is no help for it except to create an inner refuge, sited where your consciousness lives. This is the ultimate shelter. The cost is nil. No construction of wood and nails will prove as snug, or as easy to maintain. The door remains open at all hours and inside you'll always find a heartwarming fire always lit. This is home for all eternity.

BANISHING BOREDOM

Boredom is a bug-a-boo that haunts the winter of our years. (It's also the bane of most mothers' existence.) This is a state of mind (not a state of being) that is easily remedied if its cause is understood. Unfortunately, it is misunderstood by practically everyone except Richard Carlson who says,

"Boredom is caused by a busy mind."

You, and most everybody else, are wont to connect boredom to a lack of anything (enough things) to do. So, of course, when you're feeling bored, you look elsewhere, for something else ... for more stimulus. Wrong.

More is less.

The fact is, the busier your mind, the further you retreat from the present moment. As Carlson suggests, boredom is a condition produced by an over active mind. The more things that are going on at the moment, the less able you are to enjoy the moment; to stop and smell the flowers.

What's more boring that being stuck in a traffic jam.

There's no lack of things going on around you: horns honking; pedestrians crossing; lights changing; billboards advertising. And there's no lack of things to do while you're waiting: There's the radio, cassette player, a cellular phone, maybe. TIME Magazine to glance at.

184

A briefcase of homework to riffle through. A speech to practice. And yet ... you're bored.

Sitting there, your mind starts visiting all the places it would rather be. You think of all the things you'd rather be doing. That's the problem right there. You're sitting there *doing* nothing; *accomplishing* nothing. When the delay is over with, you'll have nothing to show for it. It's time wasted.

A sad testimony, that. It's a malady rife throughout the Western world, but nowhere so much as here in America, the go-go capitol.

That's why our retirement towns are jam-packed with activities; all of them based on doing; accomplishing: arts and crafts; exercise programs and dieting regimes; contests and tournaments. If one thing starts to bore you, there's always another activity waiting in the wings. No rest for the weary. Just go do it. 12 hours a day into the night. You can't take a relaxing cruise anymore. Now you've got to learn something aboard. How to invest. How to skeet shoot. How to be a chess champion. All this to banish boredom.

A misery of choice

The fact is, there can be too much on your palette. Too many choices. As soon as we choose one, we wonder if there isn't something else we should be doing. Our culture expects too much of us.

If you were marooned on that proverbial desert isle where your options were limited and nothing was expected of you, your days would be filled with observing the heavens, the waves, the shoreline, the granules of sand.

The only thing missing from that idyll is human contact.

Loneliness is not another word for boredom, but for many people it causes boredom. Some people, to be sure, are more self-sufficient than others. Give a writer, an artist or a musician the tools of their trade and days can go by before they notice they're alone.

While there's no excuse for boredom, loneliness is not so easily solved, especially late in life when by choice or necessity you are not flowing with the mainstream. The infirmities of age can leave you going around in circles in some obscure eddy. This is the time of life when your inner resources must be called into play to replace external stimuli. It is the time to create your own world, and to enjoy the creations of others — in words, music and pictures.

PRESS ON, REGARDLESS

Young people are always amazed that the elderly "keep on keeping on." At seventy or eighty, why read TIME Magazine? Why be concerned with global politics, environmental threats, future trends? Why take up a hobby that can never be perfected? Why take pride in your appearance and moderate your habits? Indeed, why even bother to get up in the morning? What's the point at that point?

In the first place, it's not over until that fat lady sings. And no one in the audience knows when that will be.

Even then, there will be other acts on other stages, but that's not the issue here.

The issue here is that indefatigable, indomitable, never-say-die spirit that keeps some people tall in the saddle with a purpose while others lie about in the barn complaining of saddle sores.

Why the lights go out for some people when they round the bend that takes them into old age, while others turn the corner at full trot ablaze with energy is not simply explained. It's not some secret you stumble across in your September years. It's a matter of caring, and caring requires purpose/meaning which is a product of your past; something you build into your life a brick at a time.

Those whose quests are never ended know nothing is ever finished; the war is never won; every battle must be refought for different reasons on different fields.

To be sure, there comes a time when Nature whispers something in our ear (no one knows what ... until it's your ear) signalling it's time to hang up your helmet and retreat to the rear to await further instructions. In the meantime, life is tumultuous; we are always losing and regaining our balance, whether on a personal or cosmic scale. So it is not winning that matters but our willingness and readiness to (re)join the battle. "Once more into the breech, Horatio ..."

Perhaps 'battle' is not the best metaphor. The 86-year old widower who takes pride in his appearance belongs in the same company. It may be he's still trying to impress others, but its more likely he's motivated by a dignity rooted in self-worth. On its face, it would be understandable if he wore the same shirt, food stains and all, 10 days running.

Who's looking? The answer, of course, is *he is!*

(IM)PATIENCE

One of the (many) qualities seniors have in common with juniors is a lack of patience, albeit for much different reasons.

Young people's impatience is due in part to their lack of experience—i.e., everything that's happened to them has happened quickly. In the short span of two or three years teenagers go though changes the likes of which they won't encounter again until the flipside of puberty —the fifties! On TV they witness lifetimes compressed into 30-minutes minus commercials! Jets flash them across a continent that required three months of unimaginable hardship for their great grandparents to traverse. So, naturally-enough, they expect everything to happen (SNAP!) like that.

People your age have their own set of excuses for showing impatience. The most palpable being your fore-shortened future. As time runs short, so does patience. Set-backs are not easily accepted. After a lifetime of bid-ing your time, you want to take the bit in your teeth and run. Autumn is no time for dawdling. 'Now or never' be-comes an imperative.

If impatience relative to time may be forgiven, what about impatience with others? The atypical senior citizen's patience is easily lost when it comes to accom-modating other people's agendas, or methods. While the time imperative is a factor; this has rather more to do with experience—too much of it. Whatever someone does (for us), we are likely to have seen it done faster and/or better in our day. We can spot mistakes in the making, and rather than let it happen, we're inclined to intervene. "No, no, **no** ... here's how you do it." Our 'crotchety' reputation is most often earned.

These proclivities usually diminish late in the game as Mother Nature loosens our grip on wheel of life. But right now, at fiftysomething, you don't have the patience to hear about that.

AGED IS A 4-LETTER WORD

The title of this piece was lifted from a 70s column in the Los Angeles TIMES authored by the venerable Jack Smith who was searching for an acceptable replacement for that ubiquitous and much-maligned phrase, senior citizen.

In any other time/culture 'senior citizen' would not be something to avoid. Heck, in Japan they even have a national holiday honoring the seniors in their society. (But that's a subject addressed elsewhere.)

Any acceptable substitute for the old standby, 'senior citizen' would necessarily be sans 'old.' For among other reasons, 'old' is relative, being neither absolute nor definitive. As Edward Gans observed, "... all of us are growing older. Some of us are simply growing older than others. There is no line we cross between 'not old' and 'old.'" Indeed, 'old' is only legitimate when referring to a point in time yet to arrive. Thus the fifties might be said to be the gateway to old (as syndicated columnist Peg Greenfield in fact said). That's okay because the interested reader is not there yet. But when it comes time to hang a sign around your neck age-dating you, there needs be some title that is neither relative nor divisive.

The above mentioned Jack Smith turned thumbs down on 'elders,' thinking it sounds too biblical (whereas 'seniors' is too collegiate, 'aging' too meaningless, and 'old' too old.)

True, we already have words that differentiate between folks (also unacceptable because just-plain 'folks' don't live

in spa-equipped condos) more than 60 years old: sexage-
narian for those sixties, septuagenarian for the 70s, octogenarian for the 80s, nonagenarian for the 90s and centenarian
for those who make it to 100 or more. Patently, six-syllable
words ain't going to make it in a society given to short-cuts.

Smith goes on to suggest his own system of shortcuts,
as being perfectly acceptable abbreviations: Sexos for the
sixties, septos for the seventies and so on—octos, nonas,
and centos. These at least have the advantage of being
short, plain, and easy to say and remember.

But what about the collective category covered by the
much-maligned 'senior citizen?' Our quoted authority
makes the following suggestion: *generian*. Not bad. Not
good, but not bad, either.

If the above strikes you as too frivolous, Smith offers
another alternative ... lifted from the French (who always
seem to have a word for any 'it'). Over there, persons past
sixty are considered to be in their 'third age,' or *troisieme*.
How's that for suave. It has a certain Continental flair and
verve, don't you think? You don't?!

Too fru-fru for you?

Face it—no single word or phrase is likely to please
those it refers to, simply because, in this culture, anything
that distances you from young is unacceptable.

And into the vacuum rushes the handy old standby,
'senior citizen.' At least it's accurate. You are, after all, a
citizen. And you clearly are not of the junior variety.

So, it would seem you're stuck with it. Unless you have
a better suggestion ...

FOR WOMYN ONLY

The author has made a conscious effort to prevent gender bias from wagging these pages. But being of the male persuasion, an in-born p.o.v. no doubt has crept in between the lines causing consternation and confusion, or just plain indignation, amongst 'the other half.'

There is little to be done about this 'cept to acknowledge, apologize and compensate in some small way with the following thoughts and considerations (of concern to women only).

While men and women share many if not most of the same concerns viz. aging, the female species to be sure is affected in ways males can only imagine. Some of those ways were mentioned in Chapter III—e.g., men tend to become more cautious and circumspect as they gray, turning inward. Also, it is generally conceded that men are more fearful of aging than women are, but talk less of it. Indeed, talking about themselves is still very difficult for most men, despite the best efforts of Robert Bly, Sam Keen, et al. Research has determined fear of death for some reason is twice as high for men than women. And while both men and women agree that 'more freedom' is what they enjoy most about growing older, the two sexes have very different ways of celebrating their new-found freedom.

Men, we have seen, tend to pull back and withdraw, while you ladies are inclined to reach-out and open-up. Men—especially successful men—are inclined to take on too much and burn-out too soon. Womenfolk don't perceive themselves as slowing down in their fifties and sixties. That's when many if not most get up to speed (leaving Harry in the dust). The woman who spent the last 30 years tending the nest may go back to school, start a day care center, cruise the Caribbean in search of scented evenings and steel bands or take a job. Or a lover. Or all of the above!

Viva la difference!

As Chapter III acknowledged, these differences are being erased as more and more working couples approach the big Five-O. But many of the divergent paths taken by older men and women are not caused by our culture but are biological in nature, namely menopause.

When the woman exits that gauntlet, there is a palpable sense of freedom—it's all downhill thereafter.

She's paid her dues and now's the time to pick up the benefits, number one of which is the time to pursue a selfish agenda.

So why do so many of you ladies end up flat on your face kicking and screaming?

One reason may be Helen Gurley Brown whose SEX AND THE SENIOR WOMAN urges you to continue to compete with other women (the majority of whom, presumably, are younger!) for the hoary prize of men's sexual attention.

A letter to the NY TIMES from a spokesperson for the Association For Women In Psychology begged to disagree. "To encourage women to try harder to appeal to the culturally-conditioned sexual desires of men only exposes (women) to the possibility of further humiliation not to say rage at men who reject them and women who have them."

A broader reply may be found in a book published in the late '80s, CROSS SECTIONS (Wm Morrow & Co.). Author Elizabeth Janeway says it may be downhill all the way, but a lack of road signs causes too many women hit the brakes. According to Janeway, there are no directions, no approved routes for women to take in the second half of their lives — only Oil Of Olay ads and advice from the likes of Helen Gurley Brown about how-to-stay-young-and-sexy-forevermore.

THE OTHER HALF

Like most women, I spent the first half of my life responding to the needs of others. One of the good things about the period ahead is that the world now makes fewer demands on me, leaving me free to pursue my own agenda; to find out who I really am.

—Neshama Franklin
from the
Chronicle Whole Earth Catalog

All alone and lonely

The lack of patterns, as well as role models, leaves the fiftysomething woman in the middle of nowhere without a map. That leads to a kind of invisibility. You're left with the feeling you face the future alone.

Janeway, and many another soulmate (among them, Betty Friedan), offer prescriptions to ameliorate this problem. But not the Bandaids of old ("Be active! Learn something new! Seek self-awareness!" and other hackneyed admonitions.)

Get a life

What's needed is a solid social context; a redefinition of female maturity, along with new social networks. These will take time to emerge. In the meantime, mid-life women must invent the rest of their lives. Granted, it's not very fair that after society has jerked you around for fiftysomething years, it leaves you hanging by the heels. But there you are. Either you will continue to twist in the breeze, or you'll get a new life. If your mate makes that impossible, dump him. Strong medicine, but we're talking survival here. You can't succeed if you don't survive.

IS THIS SHOW NECESSARY?

How many months, even years, have you spent in front of a television set? Chances are, more that half of the time you were watching that illuminated rectangle passively; that is, with little or no interest in the goings-on.

The TV has become a lamp; something you turn on when you come home; a sign that you have taken occupancy; the modern means of establishing your 'territorial imperative.' It has become part of the universal hum; a new kind of Musak. Half the time no one's even in the room watching the damn thing. Much of the rest of the time you may be watching but you certainly aren't consciousness of seeing. It's just a substitute for sucking your thumb. To make matters worse, you probably have the evening paper spread out on your lap (or maybe this book!) reading little snatches of text between glances at the box, not really comprehending either. My, how those wasted moments add up! A wasted hour is a wasted hour, no matter when you waste it: as a teenager or an octogenarian. But at this end of life, we have less excuse for squandering time. Now is the time to manage your time; to eliminate meaningless moments.

People who are often alone use the TV the way their parents used the radio: for company, as a backdrop to other domestic activities, like cooking, eating, cleaning, dressing. For single people it's almost like having a live-in companion. Sounds reasonable, but the effect is no less compromising viz. time management.

One way to break the TV habit is to mount a little sign atop your set reading, "Am I Really Enjoying This?" or, "Is This Show *Really* Necessary?" to remind you to be selective. There is something triumphant about switching off the set in the middle of some trashy sitcom or sensational expose that panders to prejudice or validates violence. It will amaze you how quickly you can digest a newspaper when you're not dividing your attention between it and 60 MINUTES. Try it. Even at this late date, being selective will add a couple of years to your life.

SECRETS OF TIME MANAGEMENT

Doing more with less

As our life expectancy shortens, the list of things to do seems to increase in inverse proportion. There are all those books to read, and the book you were always going to write. All those places to see; people to visit; classes to take; pictures to paint; gardens to plant; roofs to mend; cars to fix; basements to rearrange; attics to clean; albums to fill; restaurants to try; investments to consider; talents to develop; movies to see; magazines to scan; letters to write; ad nauseam.

Everyone's response to this misery of choice is different. For some, time management means being more selective; setting priorities: eliminating what is less important in order to leave time for what is more important. Eminently rational, but there goes spontaneity. Playing the hatchet-man to your every whim and desire isn't a fun way to spend your time.

For others it means rushing; frantic activity—never mind that nothing gets done very well. But life is more than a checklist. At this point, quality not quantity should be the measure.

Still others just throw in the towel and head for the hammock.

Down with 'downtime'

A better approach might be to eliminate 'down time,' those wasted moments (that occur between the meaningful ones) you spend in limbo accomplishing absolutely nothing. Were you to hold a stopwatch to a day in your life, chances are you'd find maybe a third of every waking hour is spent idling (different from idylling!). Of course, most people see themselves as continually busy; rushing here, hurrying there. When the dust settles, they're usually to be found standing in the same place.

Eliminating downtime has everything to do with efficiency, that which makes for effectiveness. It's more a knack than technique.

To be sure, the efficient execution of a skill, requires technique. Waiting on tables, for example. In any large restaurant, every waiter or waitress is given the same number of tables to serve. And yet invariably you'll find one who is rushing all over the place; frantically playing catch-up. While another, with no less to do, seems to have all the time in the world. He/she chats with the customers; hobnobs with the kitchen staff; has time to sneak a smoke. The one who accomplishes least works the hardest. Because every move is a study in wasted motion. Bringing the salads without the extra dressing.

The role of role models

Life is not a job, however. Or rather, life consists of many jobs. Most of the time we waste is wasted between jobs. Rest and recreation are not a waste of time—if you are really resting or recreating. But most of that 'tween time is spent preparing yourself to do something else; or cleaning up after your last effort—*i.e.* backing, filling, and pfutzing.

Eliminating that 'downtime' requires not so much technique as example. To become one of those rare people who waste not a minute yet don't appear rushed, you had best observe one in action; someone who sweeps all those wasted moments into a recycling bin that turns them into intensely meaningful hours.

We all have encountered these wunderkins somewhere in our past: people who pack an extraordinary number of experiences and accomplishments into an ordinary day and lifetime—e.g., a polo-playing Formula-I driver with homes on three continents each plastered with paintings done while recuperating from a tiger bite sustained when returning from an Everest expedition that was being filmed for National Geographic. They are at once a source of inspiration and invidious comparisons. One such fellow insists this ability has nothing to do with genes and everything to do with consciousness.

This friend of a friend has been, at different times, a child psychologist, a gynecologist and a surgeon (not necessarily in that order), as well as an accomplished ventriloquist, a talent he developed in order to communicate with autistic children. This medical Michelangelo is a sculptor of some note, a gourmand, bon vivant, and according to some knowing reports, a bit of a womanizer (a gentleman with a high regard for womankind). And when

he isn't being any of the above, he's a well-traveled jour-
nalist cum political commentator whose byline has ap-
peared in sundry high-brow, left-leaning periodicals and
esoteric journals. Between articles and 'expert' appearances on innumerable televised forums, he may be found
deep in the heart of Caribbean jungles pursuing his interest in Voodoo. The man is also an activist and on the
Board of myriad Good Causes; a much sought-after After Dinner Speaker, and the life of every newsworthy
party on both sides of the tracks on either coast.

When asked, "How do you manage it? You may be
more brilliant and talented than the rest of us, with a
higher energy level and a different metabolism ... but
not that much more—not enough to explain how you
squeeze 10-times more into your life than any of the rest
of us."

Waste not, want not

He didn't disagree. "If I have a secret," he confided,
"it's the ability to utilize every moment of every day."
He offered, as an example, the following case in point.
"On my way home after a hard day's surgery, I listen to
a cassette that helps me perfect my Swahili. Arriving at
my manse, I enter the foyer where a bust I'm working
on awaits atop its pedestal. Lifting the damp cloth, I
tweak it here and nudge it there, resulting in a finished piece in two or three month's time ... time that
otherwise would have been put to no good use." What's
more," he went on to explain, "whilst nudging and

tweaking I also giving his houseboy a shopping list for a dinner party to be attended by guests I'd invited using my cellular phone enroute to the hospital that morning."

In the time it took him to reveal his 'secret' the good doctor concocted two Mai Tais and a Ramos Fizz for three gorgeous ladies, all single, at his poolside bar, a fitting accompaniment to bruncheon platters heaped with *Huevos Rancheros* he'd whipped up a moment before.

DISCLAIMER

The good doctor may have a knack/technique for managing time, but that isn't to say he is an integrated personality. On the face of it, he appears to be a compulsive overachiever driven by who-knows what kinds of psychological problems. He is cited here not for his character; not even his accomplishments, but simply for an ability to utilize his allotment of hours. Conspicuously missing from his schedule was time spent in contemplative or spiritual pursuits. Whether or not he used his time to the best advantage, who's to say. But use it he did.

"Waste not, want not," he said, executing a flawless kickturn at the far end of his pool en route to his daily quota of laps.

A follow-up interview found him tending hothouse orchids accompanied by Sibelius, after which he repaired to a Solarium cum Observatory to do stretching exercises while maintaining his tan.

People like this are hard to take. Though they no doubt have feet of clay and suffer unknown private miseries, there is no denying they are masters of time. Neither is the explanation to be found in their material advantages as these are effects, not causes. You may lack an Aston Martin with cellular phone, a foyer and houseboy to do your bidding, but if you have a garden, why not water with a book in hand facing a westering sun. When it's time for the McNeal-Lehrer News Hour, don't just sit there—mount the exercise cycle. Life's too short to do one thing at a time.

S-E-X AND SENESCENCE

Except for the odd oblique reference, **S-E-X** is a subject conspicuously missing from this 'manual,' for the same reason there is no mention of nutrition, investment strategies, and best-buys in RVs. That reason being, there is a superfluity of books on those subjects.

There are a couple of lessor reasons this writing follows a course less travelled viz. the subject of sex.

One, at fiftysomething, there is no lack of sex. (If you were getting it in your forties, nothing's likely to change in your fifties.) And while the menfolk may harbor a fear of losing their manhood later in life, this is not a subject that's high on their list of things to worry about right now. (Womenfolk, it is patently obvious, harbor no fear of losing their womanhood, having only recently discovered the joy of sex begins après menopause!) Sex after sixty is more an expression of affection than self-gratification. And as one septuagenarian observed, "We are better at it having had more practice."

Two, if there is anything that separates this book from the growing number of other books about the 50+ years, it's a consciousness that this is the time of life to discover there's more to life than 'eat, drink and make Mary (or Harry).' This does not mean sex is unimportant at this or any other age. It's just a matter of emphasis, okay?

PREDISPOSITION VERSUS PRECOGNITION

As mentioned elsewhere, the older we are, the more we are wont to peer around corners. Also mentioned is the effect age has on our willingness to abrogate decision-making to outside forces ... to avoid responsibility by depending on 'signs.'

The age-old yearning to foretell the future has spawned all manner of arcane and occult arts, as well as some respected professions. The future that concerns these arts and sciences is limited to earth time, our terrestrial future. Thus we or our progeny will live to see the day when the soothsayers' predictions are proved true or false.

When it comes to foreseeing what's lies beyond the terrestrial horizon, we are in the hands of priests and mystics. There is no way on earth we can ever know if these spiritual guides have it right; whether God is a Catholic, a Moslem, or a Unified Theory. Perhaps that is why there are more clerics than Oracles.

Astrology revisited

Of all the predictive arts and sciences; none is so ancient, persistent and pervasive as Astrology. Certainly none is so controversial. Mention the word 'astrology' in a crowded room, and half the crowd will head for the door while the other half crowds around the speaker, adding anecdotes.

Those of you who are inclined to leave the discussion of astrology to the Shirley MacLaine contingent, are invited to stick around long enough to separate fact from fiction. (There is plenty of both to sift through, and anyone unwilling to consider the evidence can hardly be considered a 'reasonable' person.)

It is simplistic nonsense to say planetary influences make a man "assertive, independent and a pioneer." However, there are combinations of cosmic forces that could predispose an individual to develop those tendencies.

No one disputes that man is affected by his environment. And the cosmos certainly must be included in that environment.

It also is indisputable that cosmic forces recur in cyclical patterns. Statistics leave no doubt that the circadian cycle causes twice as many women to go into labor around midnight than around noon, and the peak in births occur at about 4 in the morning when the metabolic cycle is lowest and the mother is most relaxed. It is no coincidence that police choose the dogwatch, just before the dawning, to arrest and interrogate suspects.

We also have a natural tendency to respond to the circannual cycle. Children born in May, for-example, are, on the average 200 grams heavier than those born in any other month — a difference caused by an annual rhythm in the production of hormones during pregnancy. (We seem to still have a breeding season.) This situation is of course reversed in the Southern Hemisphere.

Statistics also show those born in March live an average of four years longer than those who debut any other month; while people born in May scored higher in IQ tests.

As man is 98% water, it is little wonder than the moon affects our personality as well as our physiology.

To begin with, more births occur during the waning moon than the waxing moon; with the highest number being at the time of high tide when the moon is directly overhead. It should not escape notice that the average length of the female cycle is almost identical to the period between full moons. The time of ovulation also is connected with the moon, and the ability to conceive coincides with the phase of the moon that prevailed when she was born.

That the moon induces or reduces bleeding there no longer is any doubt. 82% of all bleeding crises happen between the first and last quarters of the moon, with a significant peak when the moon is full. Indeed, more than a few surgeons prefer to operate on dark nights.

We all know the affect a full moon has on mental balance. Like so much good science, the connection between the moon and madness began as a superstition. This didn't prevent English law from distinguishing, 200 years ago, between those who were 'insane' (meaning chronically and incurably psychotic) and those who were 'lunatic' (meaning susceptible to aberrations produced by the moon). Crimes committed during the full moon were dealt with more leniently. Superintendents of asylums often cancel staff leave during a full moon when the inmates go 'loony.' The American Institute of Medical Climatology has published a report on the effect a full moon has on human behavior in which it reports crimes with psychotic motivation—arson, kleptomania, homicidal alcoholism—peak when the moon is full, and that cloudy nights are no protection against this predilection.

If the moon affects us, the sun must play it's part. The most noticeable connection has to do with sunspots. A Russian professor of history collected correlations spanning a period of forty years and dared to suggest (during the Soviet period) that major social changes are due more to this solar activity than dialectical materialism. Other research claims that the great plagues that swept Europe as well as the small pox epidemics of Chicago all occurred at the peaks of the sun's 11-year cycle. The same research points out there were Liberal governments in power in England during sunspot peaks while the Conservatives reigned only in quieter years. There is convincing evidence that changes in blood serum occur mainly when sunspots interfere with the earth's magnetic field, and that solar radiation promotes the formation of blood clots. And, indeed, hemorrhages in the lungs of tubercular patients follow this pattern, with the most dangerous days being those when the Aurora Borealis can be seen.

These sun-induced changes in the earth's magnetic field also has an affect on the nervous system. A study of more than 5,000 coal mine accidents shows that most occur on the day following solar activity. A survey of more than 28,000 admissions to psychiatric hospitals showed there's a marked increase on days when observatories reported strong solar activity.

Astrology is based on the premise that celestial phenomena affect life and events here on earth. There are few scientists, and no biologists knowledgeable on weather and other cycles who deny this premise. The only argument is the matter of degree and whether you should factor this into your plans for the day.

Rather than being mere pawns in some celestial crap game, we remain, at whatever age, captains of our own destiny. Free will can overcome the sum total of influences, both inherited and environmental. Each and every day we must step up to the plate, carrying the bat of our choice, and face whatever fate throws in your direction.

TEACHING OLD DOGS NEW TRICKS

It's what you learn after you know it all that counts.
—Proverb

Most people are open to learning and growing. It would follow that they enjoy the process. (Those who do not are not likely to be reading this, thus there is no need to accommodate them!)

If there is a time of life when we are most open to this process it is when we are children and know nothing, and again late in life when we know it all. At fiftysomething we have accumulated all the available conventional wisdom. Now we're ready to enroll in a postgraduate course in Lifesmanship. It's an open-ended study program; that is, there is no end to it. The subjects covered have no practical application. Your gain will be measured in dignity, forbearance, a hard-headed optimism, good humor, an indefatigable vitality, along with a 360° perspective that enables you to maintain your balance no matter what life throws at you.

MID-LIFE CRISIS CONTROL

If you listen to gerontologists, gynecologists, and other medical mediators you'll hear nothing good about middle-age. That's because doctors only see sick, crisis-prone people—i.e., **patients!** All the well ones are somewhere else having a good time beyond the reach of medically-funded researchers.

In realty, the vast majority of fiftysomething men and women come to terms with middle-age through a long and gentle, more or less natural process.

If Carl Jung was correct to divide life into two halves, the first being devoted to 'making it' or **becoming,** and the second to 'enjoying it' or **being,** the shift from one to the other is bound to create changes we are apt to call 'losses,' whether its in terms of physical prowess, relationships or purpose. Most of us turn these losses into gains: We find a larger meaning for the fifty years of effort and redirect our competitive spirit from the corporation to the community.

The people who end up in doctors' offices are those who react to these external losses with denial, fear, or a sense of defeat. The most common is denial, refusing to acknowledge limitations. They still feel pressured to conform to a youthful stereotype; their dreams run counter to reality. There is little in common between the inner and outer person. If they do come to terms with the realities of middle-age, it'll be an 11th hour transformation, acute and painful, the stuff that keeps the health care industry busily engaged.

212

MAKING BELIEVE

One of the joys of youth was daydreaming, imagining yourself a rock star or rocket scientist, taking a Victory Lap at Indianapolis, being entangled in the arms of some irresistible movie star, raising the Winner's Cup at Wimbledon, you name it. At that age all things were possible.

As we grow older, our options are reduced and so is the time we spend making-believe. Remembering replaces anticipation. The harsh realities imposed by a foreshortened future put a damper on daydreaming, leaving us with no castles in the sky. We daren't fantasize about sex, or imagine ourselves becoming a millionaire or, Heaven forbid, a movie star. Pity.

No wonder nothing magical happens late in life. Making believe something is possible makes it possible. Pretending is a necessary preliminary to **doing**. As Francis Bacon née Shakespeare once said, "We are such stuff as dreams are made on." So dream on.

FROM HERE TO ETERNITY

The religious concept of 'eternal life' implies endless time; going on year after year forevermore. An everlasting continuum.

Barns in the Bible Belt often are emblazoned with the enigmatic question, "Where will you spend eternity?"

An odd question in that 'spending' implies a finite quantity (of time).

On the face of it, that view of eternity is absurd.

Eternity is not a given *quantity* of time: It transcends time, being a *qualitative* concept, a way of relating to life rather than a series of ethereal tomorrows.

Here again, the issue is *time*, and its relativity to past time and future time. Part'n'parcel of this issue is immortality.

Jesus proclaimed, "the Kingdom of Heaven is within you." He was saying, eternity is to be found in the way you relate to each given moment.

Presumably the reader has reached that time of life when the thought of dying encourages you to take the present seriously; to replace quantitative time with the qualitative variety. And quality moments require you to live consciously, aware of your self as the actor, director and producer of this epic called 'Your Life.'

BEYOND WORDS

This book has not been written to a certain mind set re: spiritual matters. The readers' one and only common denominator is age ... along with the cultural commonalities shared by your generation. There is little else in the way of like-mindedness the author can lean on. Some of you include the 'Born Again,' while others haven't been born once when it comes to an abiding religious belief. Having grown up in the 60s, no doubt many of you have been inoculated with New Age cum Aquarian values; not to forget those who find their Greater Power manifested in Nature.

This variegated constituency presents a writer with quite a challenge. There is no avoiding the Eternal Verities when discussing age; yet one man's truth is another's blasphemy. The problem is compounded by the essential illusiveness of the subject, and the vagaries of language and usage.

Words are like globs of damp clay, so full of possibilities, so willing to be molded into something resembling a thought or image. Yet so resistant to reality.

For both the artist and writer, there is much slippage 'twixt the mind and the fingertip (that executes the mind's commands). This is due partly to the inherent limitations of language, and partly to the limitations of those manipulating the symbols that comprise language.

These limitations are never so evident as when used to describe transcendent subjects. Matters of the spirit, like a state of mind, cannot be pictured directly as can a material object. You cannot take a pencil and picture fear for instance. You cannot take a brush and paint remorse, or envy, or sensuality as such. Justice, too, is an abstract quality. You are driven to adopt allegories: a blindfolded woman holding balanced scales. Something concrete to express inner, subjective ideas. The Bible is chock-a-block with symbols and allegories, starting with Adam and Eve: Adam means the body, and Eve means the soul or human mind.

Certainly there is nothing more illusive than spiritual ideas that have no definable shape or other known qualities. How to describe that which no one has ever objectively experienced? What criteria can the reader use to test the validity of the writer's writing?

In the same fashion that poetry owes more to feelings than meanings, inspirational writing must, of necessity, soar above the rational plane. And once in that rarefied atmosphere, there are emotions and experiences but no facts to discipline the writer.

The poet who speaks of universalities like love and motherhood is on firmer ground. While love can neither be weighed nor measured, it is an emotion we all can recognize and relate to.

Matters of the spirit are more illusive, as well as emotionally-charged. As such, they are riven with opposing points of view; each defended with a passion that can over-ride the instinct for survival.

God is variously described as a He with a beard, alternately loving and wrathful; forgiving and vengeful. To the quantum physicist, God is the originating, primordial energy. To the naturalist, God is Nature. He has as many personas as mansions. To followers of Islam, God is Allah. Members of New Guinea's Cargo Cult see God as a C-46 transport plane disgorging parachutes loaded with manna. Those attending AA meetings prefer 'Greater Power.'

When speaking of mind/soul/spirit/consciousness, much less of a state of awareness existing independent of the body, is to invite all manner of criticism and complaint. The writer who would do so must be prepared for assaults on his jugular as well as his mother, wife, homeland and Alma Mater.

That hasn't stopped billions of people from writing and talking about Heaven and Hell. A few million of those billions are attracted to the subject precisely because of its vagaries. They cannot be proved wrong. Which generates a good deal of absolutism. Theirs is not to reason-why but to proclaim, "Follow me into the unknown ... I know the way!"

Writers must necessarily employ reason to bridge the chasm separating the finite from the infinite. Thus they are immediately confronted with a predicament in which reason would despair. In frustration, many have written of that:

> *We can never find true language to express Heaven and God, since one is a state of consciousness and the second infinity.*

*Language undoubtedly assisted the growth of rea-
son, the exchange of ideas, the initiation and spread
of new inventions, and the enlargement of the cerebral cortex, but it might also have repressed a more
primitive form of knowing.*

*Words are cantankerous contrivances; vague when
we need them precise; ambiguous when we need
them—yet the only tool for forming a community.*

*To accurately convey this conception in words is
perhaps impossible, and to attempt definition is to
introduce that very idea of limitation which is our
object to avoid.*

One who would write in the metaphysical metaphor
faces still another block. He treads in giant footsteps,
having been proceeded by all the Great Ones; by Testa-
ments Old and New. The only justification for adding
one word to this record is the hope it is a word that will
move someone closer to the truth. For if the architect of
heaven and earth resides in many mansions, there must
be many paths thereto, some paved with prose, some
with poetry, with myriad authors contributing the stepping stones.

AMEN

The following words of wisdom (source unknown), framed as a prayer, should be repeated daily by anyone past the age of fifty:

Lord, thou knowest better than I know myself that I am growing older and someday soon will be well and truly aged. Keep me from growing talkative and particularly from the fateful habit of thinking I must say something on every subject and every occasion. Release me from craving to try to straighten out everyone's affairs. Keep my mind from recital of endless detail; give me wings to get to the point. I ask for grace enough to listen to the tales of others' pains. But seal my lips on my own. They are increasing, and my love of rehearsing them is becoming sweeter with each passing year (what my wife calls organ recitals). Teach me the glorious lesson that occasionally I might possibly be mistaken. Keep me reasonably sweet. I do not wish to be a saint for they are not easily lived with. Make me thoughtful, but not moody; helpful but not bossy for I want a few friends at the end.

Amen.

OTHER WORDS ON
AGE & AGING

It's all right to be a late bloomer if you don't miss the flower show.

—Anonymous

———≡◆≡———

At the end of every road you meet your self.

—S.N. Behrman

———≡◆≡———

*For they hear the wind laugh and
murmur and sing
Of a land where even the old
are fair
And even the wise are merry
of tongue.*

—William Butler Yeats
The Land of Heart's Desire

———≡◆≡———

*The first forty years of life give us the text: the next thirty supply the
commentary.*

—Schopenhauer

There is more felicity on the far side of baldness than young men can possibly imagine.

—L.P. Smith

No wise man ever wished to be younger.

—Swift

Every generation is a secret society and has incommunicable enthusiasms, tastes, and interests which are a mystery both to it predecessors and to posterity.

—Chapman

Youth is a blunder; manhood a struggle; old age a regret.

—Disraeli

Senescence begins
And middle age ends
The day your descendants
Outnumber your friends.

—Nash

221

A man of fifty is responsible for his face.

—Stanton

There is no cure for birth and death save to enjoy the interval.

—Santayana

An old man concludeth from his knowing mankind
that they know him too, and that maketh him very wary.

—Halifax

I've never known a person to live to 110 or more, to be remarkable for
anything else.

—Billings

One of the two things that men who have lasted for a hundred years
always say: either that they have drunk whiskey and smoked all
their lives, or that neither tobacco nor spirits ever made the faintest
appeal to them.

—Lucas

MOPPING UP

Few envy the consideration enjoyed by the eldest inhabitant.
—Emerson

Nothing is more beautiful than cheerfulness in an old face.
—Richter

Next to the very young, I suppose the very old are the most selfish.
—Thackeray

After the age of eighty, all contemporaries are friends.
—Mme. De Dino

All men are born truthful, and die liars.
—Vauvenargues

Death is that after which nothing is of interest.
—Rozinov

TIME HAPPENS

It is death, and not what comes after death, that men are generally afraid of.

—Samuel Butler

Old age is always 15 years older than you are.

—Bernard Baruch

How old would you be if you didn't know how old you was?

—Satchel Paige

Youth is America's oldest tradition

—Oscar Wilde

One thing only has been lent to youth and age in common—discontent.

—Mathew Arnold

Only young people need new friends.

—Art Hoppe

—the last of life for which the first was made.
>—Eliz. Browning

Youth would be an ideal state if it came much later in life.
>—Lord Asquith

Endure life's indignities with dignity.
>—John W. Gardner

Age doesn't make you boring,
Boring makes you boring.
>— from 'Taking My Turn'

You make a new life for yourself when you are old.
>—John Gielgud

We are always the same age inside.
>—Gertrude Stein

Let's go to hell with our top hats on.

—Anon.

I would like to live to be 90, and see a well-turned ankle, and say, like Oliver Wendell Holmes, "I wish I were 70 again."

—Chas McCabe

The body attains perfection at age 35; the soul at 50.

—Aristotle

Parting is all we know of heaven and all we need of hell.

—Emily Dickinson

Is not old wine wholesomest, old pippins toothsomest, old wood burns brightest, old linen washes whitest and old lovers are soundest.

—John Webster

At age 50, the motto might best be, **no more bullshit.**

—Gail Sheehy

*You Can No Longer Deceive YourSelves
As You Did Before.
You Now Have Got the Taste of Truth.*
                                    —Ouspensky

AUTHOR, AUTHOR !

The graying of America is a subject that leaves most writers speechless. Hardly surprising, the essential qualification being longevity.

Mr. Coombs has other qualifications, to be sure. He has been active in the human potential movement since it flowed out of the East to enter the mainstream of Western life in the halcyon 60's. Being a native of San Francisco, the Cultural Revolution's HQ, Samm did his part to raise America's consciousness a couple of notches. He co-Founded a self-realization center for young adults; an experience that inspired his phenomenally successful (4 editions, totalling more than 100,000 copies), *TEENAGE SURVIVAL MANUAL*, dealing with the flipside of the fifties. He also was behind ACT II, a workshop (now called 'Recovery Group') for the suddenly single.

The author left a blooming advertising career—he was President of one of the West Coast's leading ad agencies—to be an agent of change, launching this country's first Pro Bono Publico communications agency to help the disestablished get established.

Mr. Coombs' list of literary credits is nothing if not eclectic. He has written about dangerous avocations (*Edgework*), the environment (*The First Green Christmas*) and its sequel *The New Green Christmas*, baseball (*America's National Game*), Early California (*Wining, Dining and Reclining With The Nabobs Of Nob Hill*). Note: Halo Books will soon publish his "survival manual for parents of teenager" titled *Make Happy Music (and Happy Dancers Will Join You)*.

When he isn't writing, Mr. Coombs often may be found speaking to audiences as diverse as New Thought congregations, teenage detainees and admen.

Samm resides in Marin County with his wife, Shirley.

Editor's note: Asked about the double-m, Samm explains, somewhat enigmatically, "At 21 I decided it was time to drop the 'y.' Readers of TIME HAPPENS will agree Samm has the approached the subject of 'successful aging' in the same iconoclastic fashion.

ORDER FORM

Use this form to order additional copies of
TIME HAPPENS
and other recent Halo Books.

To: Halo Books
    P.O. Box 2529
    San Francisco, CA 94126

I enclose check/money order payable to Halo Books in the
amount of $_____for books noted on list below. (Add
$1.50 for shipping one book and $.50 for each additional book,
California residents please add 7% sales tax.)

Mail to:
Name_____
Street address_____
City_____State_____Zip_____

Please send:

____copies of *TIME HAPPENS* $13.95 per copy
      You Could Not Have Picked
      A Better Time To Be Fiftysomething

____copies of *SUDDENLY SINGLE!* $13.95 per copy
      A Lifeline For Anyone Who
      Has Lost A Love

(continued on next page)

_____copies of *IF HE LOVE ME* $12.95 per copy
     WHY DOESN'T HE TELL ME?

_____copies of *A GARDEN OF WOMAN'S* $12.95 per copy
     WISDOM. A Secret Garden
     For Renewal

_____copies of *TEENAGE SURVIVAL* $ 9.95 per copy
     MANUAL. Being in charge of
     your own mind and body.

_____copies of *AM I A HINDU?* $14.95 per copy
     The Hinduism Primer.

_____copies of *YOUR SEXUAL* $15.95 per copy
     HEALTH. What teenagers
     need to know about sexually
     transmitted diseases and
     pregnancy.

_____copies of *YOU ARE MY FRIEND.* $9.95 per copy
     A Celebration of Friendship.

_____copies of *LOVING CHILDREN.* $9.95 per copy
     Words of Love About Kids
     from Those Who Cherish Them.

For a free catalog of all Halo Books in print, write the address above.

Retailers should order from their wholesaler or Halo's national distributor, Atrium Publishing Group, PO Box 108, Lower Lake, CA 95457. Telephone 1-800-275-2606.

Thank you.